Bible Study for
Young Adults
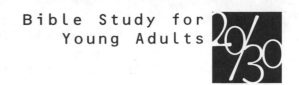

ABUNDANCE

Living Responsibly
With God's Gifts

D1622783

John W. Peterson

Abingdon Press
Nashville

Abundance: Living Responsibly With God's Gifts

20/30: Bible Study for Young Adults

by John W. Peterson

Copyright © 2001 by Abingdon Press

ISBN 0-687-09143-8

This book is printed on acid-free paper.

MANUFACTURED IN THE UNITED STATES OF AMERICA.

03 04 05 06 07 08 09 00—10 9 8 7 6 5 4 3 2

CONTENTS

MEET THE WRITER

A graduate of the Claremont School of Theology, the Rev. John W. Peterson is an ordained elder of the Pacific Northwest Annual Conference of The United Methodist Church. When not fortifying himself with caffeine at his local coffee haunt, John can be found earnestly writing in his home office. His work has been featured in *New World Outlook*, *Connect*, *The Lutheran*, and *Group* magazine. John also wrote the leader resource for *Fired Up! Youth Living as United Methodists Today*," a study of the history of The United Methodist Church. He contributes regularly to *LinC* (*Living in Christ*) and *FAITHLINK*, United Methodist curriculum resources that bring together the biblical witness and everyday life issues.

John's final advice for anyone burdened with excessive wealth: "Become a writer and this too shall pass."

WELCOME TO 20/30: BIBLE STUDY FOR YOUNG ADULTS

The *20/30* Bible study series is offered for post-modern adults who want to participate in and help structure their own discoveries—in life, in relationships, in faith. In each of the volumes of this series, we will have the opportunity to use our own experience in life and faith to examine the biblical texts in new ways. We will examine biblical images that shape all of our lives, even if we are not immediately aware that they do.

Image Is Everything

Images are what shape our decisions. We may think or know certain important data that weigh heavily in a decision. We may value the advice and counsel of others. We may find that the stated or implied wishes of others influence what we do. But in the end, it is often the *image* we hold that makes the decision.

For example, perhaps you were deeply hurt by someone important to you—an employer, a friend, even a pastor. You know in your heart that the institution is not to blame or that friendships are based on more than one event. But the image shaped by the difficult experience is that the job, or the friend, or the church cannot be relied upon. You *know* better, but you just have to make a change anyway. The image was more powerful than the reason.

Images are powerful, and they are familiar. In each of the studies in this series, you will encounter a well-known image that will connect your familiar experiences with some basis in Scripture.

You define for yourself what you think is "the good life." Is your definition complete? *Abundance: Living Responsibly With God's Gifts* will guide you into the biblical understanding of abundant life and help you sort out many of the faithful and practical issues that come together in a life of abundance.

You love and are loved in return, and you know this is more than just a matter of emotion. *Love: Opening Your Heart to God and Others* will guide you into the biblical understanding of love and help you explore many facets of love, and love gone wrong, with God, family, friends, and life partner.

You have faith, but may also realize that it can mean many things. Is it belief or trust, or waiting or moral behavior, or something else? Or is it all those things? *Faith: Living a Spirited Life* helps you examine your faith and grow as a Christian.

You know what it's like to make agreements, to establish commitments, to give your word and expect to be trusted. *Covenant: Making Commitments That Count* engages you in study sessions that explain a variety of covenants, what happens when covenants are broken, how to have a faithful covenant to care for others and for the earth, and certainly, what it means to have this sacred covenant with God.

You know what it is like to move to a new place, to have to deal with transitions in school or work or in relationships. You have probably experienced changes in your family as you have grown up and moved out on your own. Some of these moves are gradual, just taken in stride. Others can be painful or abrupt; certainly life-changing. In *Exodus: Leaving Behind, Moving On*, you will appreciate learning how God is in the midst of those movements, no matter how minor or how transformational.

You know how important it is to have a sense of support and roots; to have friends and a life partner. *Community: Living Faithfully With Others* introduces you to Scriptures and life examples that delve into intimacy, work, and family relationships, and more.

Experience, Faith, Growth, and Action

Each volume in this series will help you probe, on your own terms, how your experience links with your faith and how deepening your faith develops your life experience. If you need a prompt for your reflection, each volume has several pages of real-life case studies. As your faith and commitment to Jesus Christ grow, you may be looking for ways to be involved in specific service opportunities. Several are listed on pages 79-80.

We hope this series will help you encounter God through Scripture, reflection, and dialogue with others who desire to grow in faith, and to serve others. One image we hold is that God is in all things. God is certainly with you.

HOW TO USE THIS RESOURCE

Each session of this resource includes similar components or elements:
- A statement of the issue or question to be explored
- Several "voices" of persons who are currently dealing with that issue
- Exploration of biblical passages relative to the question raised
- "Biblical Studies 101" boxes that provide insight about the study of the Bible
- Questions for reflection and discussion
- Suggested individual and group activities designed to bring the session to life
- Optional case studies (found in the back of the book)
- Various service learning activities related to the session (found in the back of the book)

Choices, Choices, Choices

Collectively, these components mean one thing: *choice*. You have choices to make concerning how to use each session of this resource. Want just the nitty-gritty Bible reading, reflection, and study for personal or group use? Then focus your attention on just those components during your study time.

Like starting with real-life stories about issues then moving into how the Bible might be relevant? Start with the "voices" and move on from there. Use the "voices" to encourage group members to speak about their own experiences.

Prefer highly charged discussion encounters where many different viewpoints can be heard? Start the session with the biblical passages, followed by the questions and group activities. Be sure to compare the ideas found in the "Biblical Studies 101" boxes with your current ideas for more discussion. Want the major challenge of applying biblical principles to a difficult problem? After reading the biblical material, read one of the case studies, using the guideline provided on page 14; or get involved with one of the service learning components, described on pages 79-80.

Great Versatility

This resource has been designed for many different uses. Some persons will use this resource for personal study and reflection. Others will want to explore the work with a small group of friends. And still other folks will see this book as a different type of Sunday school resource.

Spend some time thinking about your own questions, study habits, and learning styles or those of your small group. Then use the guidelines mentioned above to fashion each session into a unique Bible study session to meet those requirements.

Highly Participatory

As you will see, the Scriptures, "voices," commentary, and experience of group members will provide an opportunity for an active, engaging time together. The greatest challenge for a group leader might be "crowd control"—being sure everyone has the chance to put his or her ideas into the mix!

The Scriptures will help you and those who study with you to make connections between real-life issues and the Bible. This resource values and encourages personal participation as a means to fully understand and appreciate the intersection of personal belief with God's ongoing work in each and every life.

ON ORGANIZING A SMALL GROUP

Learning with a small group of persons offers certain advantages over studying by yourself. First, you will hopefully encounter different opinions and ideas, making the experience of Bible study a richer and more challenging event. Second, any leadership responsibilities can be shared among group members. Third, different persons will bring different talents. Some will be deep thinkers while other group members will be creative giants. Some persons will be newcomers to the Bible; their questions and comments will help others clarify their deeply held assumptions.

So how does one go about forming a small group? Follow the steps below and see how easy this task can be.

- **Read through the resource carefully.** Think about the ideas presented, the questions raised, and the exercises suggested. If the sessions of this work excite you, it will be easier for you to spread your enthusiasm to others.

- **Spend some time thinking about church members, friends, and coworkers who might find the sessions of this resource interesting.** On a sheet of paper, list two characteristics or talents you see in each person that would make him or her an attractive Bible study group member. Some talents might include "deep thinker," "creative wizard," or "committed Christian." Remember: The best small group has members who differ in learning styles, talents, ideas, and convictions, but who respect the dignity and integrity of the other members.

- **Most functional small groups have seven to fifteen members.** Make a list of potential group members that doubles your target number. For instance, if you would like a small group of seven to ten members, be prepared to invite fourteen to twenty persons.

- **Once your list of potential candidates is complete, decide on a tentative location and time.** Of course, the details can be negotiated with those persons who accept the invitation, but you need to sound definitive and clear to perspective group members. "We will initially set Wednesday night from 7 to 9 P.M. at my house for our meeting time" will sound more attractive than "Well, I don't know either when or where we would be meeting, but I hope you will consider joining us."

- **Make initial contact with prospective group members short, sweet, and to the point.** Say something like, "We are putting together a Bible study using a different kind of resource. When would be a good time to show you the resource and talk about the study?" Establishing a special time to make the invitation takes the pressure off the prospective group member to make a quick decision.

- **Show up at the decided time and place.** Talk with each prospective member individually. Bring a copy of the resource with you. Show each person what excites you about the study and mention the two unique characteristics or talents you feel he or she would offer the group. Tell each person the initial meeting time and location and how many weeks the small group will meet. Also mention that the need for a new time or location could be discussed during the first group meeting. Ask for a commitment to come to the first session. Thank individuals for their time.

- **Give a quick phone call or e-mail to thank all persons for their consideration and interest.** Remind persons of the time and location of the first meeting.

- **Be organized.** Use the first group meeting to get acquainted. Briefly describe the seven sessions. Have a book for each group member, and discuss sharing responsibilities for leadership.

LEADING AND SHARING LEADERSHIP

So the responsibility to lead the group has fallen upon you? Don't sweat it. Follow these simple suggestions and you will razzle and dazzle the group with your expertise.

■ **Read the session carefully.** Look up all the Bible passages. Take careful notes about the ideas, statements, questions, and activities in the session. Try all the activities.

■ **Using twenty to twenty-five blank index cards, write one idea, activity, Bible passage, or question from the session on each card** until you either run out of material or cards. Be sure to look at the case studies and service learning options.

■ **Spend a few moments thinking about the members of your group.** How many like to think about ideas, concepts, or problems? How many need to "feel into" an idea by storytelling, worship, prayer, or group activities? Who are the "actors" who prefer a hands-on or participatory approach, such as an art project or simulation, to grasp an idea? List the names of all group members, and record whether you believe each to be a THINKER, FEELER, or ACTOR.

■ **Place all the index cards in front of you in the order in which they originally appeared in the session.** Looking at that order, ask yourself: 1) Where is the "head" of the session—the key ideas or concepts? 2) Where is the "heart" of the session in which persons will have a deep feeling response? 3) Where are the "feet"—those activities that ask the group to put the ideas and feelings to use? Separate the cards into three stacks: HEAD, HEART, and FEET.

■ **Now construct the "body" for your class.** Shift the cards around, using a balance of HEAD, HEART, and FEET cards to determine which activities you will do and in what order. This will be your group's unique lesson plan. Try to choose as many cards as you have group members. Then, match the cards: HEAD and THINKERS; HEART and FEELERS; FEET and ACTORS for each member of the group. Don't forget a card for yourself. For instance, if your group has ten members, you should have about ten cards.

- **Develop the leadership plan.** Invite these group members prior to the session to assist in the leadership. Show them the unique lesson plan you developed. Ask for their assistance in developing and/or leading each segment of the session as well as a cool introduction and a closing ritual or worship experience.

Your lesson plan should start with welcoming the participants. Hopefully everyone will have read the session ahead of time. Then, begin to move through the activity cards in the order of your unique session plan, sharing the leadership as you have agreed.

You may have chosen to have all the HEAD activities together, followed by the HEART cards. This would introduce the session's content, followed by helping group members "feel into" the issue through interactive stories, questions, and exercises with all group members. Feel free to add more storytelling, discussion, prayer, meditation, or worship.

You may next have chosen to use the FEET cards to end the session. Ask the group, "What difference should this session make in our daily lives?" You or the ACTORS should introduce the FEET cards as possible ways to discern a response. Ensuring that group members leave with a few practical suggestions for doing something different during the week is the point of this section of the unique lesson plan.

- **Remember: leading the group does not mean "Do it all yourself."** With a little planning, you can enlist the talents of many group members. By inviting group members to lead parts of the session that feel comfortable for them you will model and encourage shared leadership. Welcome their interests in music, prayer, worship, Bible, and so on, to develop innovative and creative Bible study sessions that can transform lives in the name of Jesus Christ.

CHOOSING TEACHING OPTIONS

This young adult series was designed, written, and produced out of an understanding of the attributes, concerns, joys, and faith issues of young adults. With great care and integrity, this image-based print resource was developed to connect biblical events and relationships with contemporary, real life situations of young adults. Its pages will promote Christian relationships and community, support new biblical learning, encourage spiritual development, and empower faithful decision-making and action.

This study is well-suited to young adults and may be used confidently and effectively. But with the great diversity within the young adult population, not every line of this study will be written "just for you." To be most relevant, some portions of the study material need to be tailored to fit your particular group. Adjustments for a good fit involve making choices from options offered by the resource. This customizing may be done easily by a designated leader who is familiar with the layout of the resource and the young adults who are using it.

What to Expect

In this study Scripture and real life images mesh together to provoke a personal response. Young adults will find themselves thinking, feeling, imagining, questioning, making decisions, professing faith, building connections, inviting discipleship, taking action, and making a difference. Scripture is at the core of each session. Scenarios weave in the dimensions of real life. Narrative and text boxes frame plenty of teaching options to offer young adults.

Each session is part of a cohesive volume, but is designed to stand alone. One session is not dependent on knowledge or experience accumulated from other sessions. A group leader can freely choose from the teaching options in an individual session without wondering about how it might affect the other sessions.

A Good Fit

For a better fit, alter the session based on what is known about the young adult participants. Young adults are a diverse constituency with varied experiences, interests, needs, and values. There is really no single defining characteristic that links young adults. Specific information about the age, employment status, household, personal relationships, and lifestyle among participants will equip a leader to make choices that ensure a good fit.

■ **Customize.** Read through the session. Notice how scenarios and teaching options move from integrating Scripture and real life dimensions to inviting a response.

■ **Look at the scenario(s).** How real is the presentation of real life? Say that the main character is a professional, white male, married, in his late twenties, and caught in a workplace dilemma that entangles his immediate superior and a subordinate from his division. Perhaps your group members are mostly college students and recent graduates, unmarried, and still on the way to being "settled." There are many differences between the man in the scenario and these group members.

As a leader, you could choose to eliminate the case study, substitute it with another scenario (there are several more choices on pages 79–80), claim the validity of the dilemma and shift the spotlight from the main character to the subordinate, or modify the description of the main character. Break-out groups based on age or employment experience might also be used to accommodate the differences and offer a better fit.

■ **Look at the teaching options.** How are the activities propelling participants toward a personal response? Perhaps the Scripture study requires more meditative quiet than is possible and a more academic, verbal, or artistic approach would offer a better fit. Maybe more direct decisions or actions would fit better than more passive or logical means. Try to keep a balance, though, that allows participants to "get out of their head" to reflect and also to move toward action.

Conceivably, there could just be too much in any one session. As a leader, you can pick and choose among teaching options, substitute case studies, take two meetings to do one session, and adapt any process to make a better fit. The tailoring process can be evaluated as adjustments are made. Judge the fit every time you meet. Ask questions that gauge relevance, and assess how the resource has stretched minds, encouraged discipleship, and changed lives.

USING BREAK-OUT GROUPS

20/30 break-out groups are small groups that encourage the personal sharing of lives and the gospel. The name "break-out" is a sweeping term that includes a variety of small group settings. A break-out group may resemble a Bible study group, an interest group, a sharing group, or other types of Christian fellowship groups.

Break-out groups offer young adults a chance to belong and personally relate to one another. Members are known, nurtured, and heard by others. Young adults may agree and disagree while maximizing the exchange of ideas, information, or options. They might explore, confront, and resolve personal issues and feelings with empathy and support. Participants can challenge and hold each other accountable to a personalized faith and stretch its links to real life and service.

Forming Break-Out Groups

The nature of these small break-out groups will depend on the context and design of the specific session. On occasion the total group of participants will be divided for a particular activity. Break-out groups will differ from one session to the next. Variations may involve the size of the group, how group members are divided, or the task of the group. Break-out groups may also be used to accommodate differences and help tailor the session plan for a better fit. In some sessions, specific group assembly instructions will be provided. For other sessions, decisions regarding the size or division of small groups will be made by the designated leader. Break-out groups may be in the form of pairs or trios, family-sized groups of three to six members, or groups of up to ten members.

They may be arranged simply by grouping persons seated next to one another or in more intentional ways by common interests, characteristics, or life experience. Consider creating break-out groups according to age; gender; type of household, living arrangements, or love relationships; vocation, occupation, career, or employment status; common or built-in connections; lifestyle; values or perspective; or personal interests or traits.

Membership

The membership of break-out groups will vary from session-to-session, or even within specific sessions. Young adults need to work at knowing and being known, so that there can be a balance between break-out groups that are more similar and those that reflect greater diversity. There may be times when more honest communication, trust, or accountability may be desired and group leaders will need to be free to self-select members for small groups.

It is important for *20/30* break-out groups to practice acceptance and to value the worth of others. The potential for small groups to encourage personal sharing and significant relationships is enhanced when members agree to exercise active listening skills, keep confidences, expect authenticity, foster trust, and develop ways of loving one another. All group members contribute to the development and function of break-out groups. Designated leaders especially need to model manners of hospitality and help ensure that each group member is respected.

Invitational Listening

Consider establishing an "invitational listening" routine that validates the perspective and affirms the voice of each group member. After a question or statement is posed, pause and allow time to think—not all persons think on their feet or talk out loud to think. Then, initiate conversation by inviting one group member, by name, to talk. This person may either choose to talk or to "pass." Either way, this person is honored and is offered an opportunity to speak and be heard. This person carries on the ritual by inviting another group member, by name, to speak. The process continues until all have been invited, by name, to talk. As each one invites another, the responsibility of acceptance and hospitality in the break-out groups is shared among all its members.

Study group members break-out to belong, to share the gospel, to care, and to watch over one another in Christian love. "So deeply do we care for you that we are determined to share with you not only the gospel of God but also our own selves, because you have become very dear to us" (1 Thessalonians 2:8).

ABUNDANCE:
LIVING RESPONSIBLY WITH GOD'S GIFTS

Who Wants to Be a Millionaire? Judging from the response to ABC's hit game show, just about everyone. Three times a week, millions of Americans tune in to watch an ordinary Joe or Jane become television's latest instant "lottery" winner. According to a Gallup poll conducted in February 2000, three out of four Americans (74 percent) have seen *Millionaire*. What's more, 240,000 of those viewers call ABC daily in hopes of getting their chance to grasp the golden ring. It is, as one television executive put it, "the American Dream."

Of course, for anyone reading the signs of the time, the success of *Millionaire* is hardly shocking. After all, Americans have gone gaw-gaw over moola! Stamp the word *money* on your product and it's sure to be hot. While television network executives are tearing out their hair trying to come up with the next *Millionaire* knock-off, the moguls of publishing are churning out truckloads of books on the subject of creating wealth. Amazon.com alone lists dozens of books with the word *millionaire* in the title, including *The Millionaire Next Door*, *The 401(k) Millionaire*, *365 Ways to Become a Millionaire*, *The Millionaire Mind*, and numerous others. There is even a lifestyle magazine entitled *Millionaire*, which recently increased its rate of publication from four to ten times a year to keep up with demand.

Gimme the Money

In short, the phenomenal success of *Who Wants to Be a Millionaire?* reflects a growing societal urgency to get a piece of the monetary pie; to become rich—not just comfortable, but filthy rich. The flower children of the 1960's have become the affluent boomers of the 21st century. America's economic engine, fueled by information technology, has gone into overdrive, creating an unprecedented explosion of wealth, including for persons in their 20s and 30s. As a result, even middle-class Americans, once satisfied with a steady wage and a secure pension, are being lured onto the fiscal rocks by the seductive siren song of the "lifestyle of the rich and famous."

They are not told by the prevailing myth of "something for nothing" they must delay their material gratification. Whereas the barons of 19th century industry spent a lifetime amassing their fortunes, today's millionaire "wanna-bees" want it now—instantly! For today's wealth isn't accumulated during a lifetime of hard work, but is an instant reward for being in the right place at the right time. "Americans don't want to wait years to get rich anymore," points out Ben Stein, host of *Win Ben Stein's Money*. "They see everybody else getting rich overnight."

Strangely Mum

Surprisingly, the church has had little to say about the epidemic of greed gripping America. Instead of offering its flock rules of economic engagement, religious institutions have remained strangely mum in the face of mammon's onslaught. Their reluctance to speak out strongly mirrors society's own. For, whereas we are now free to speak of former societal taboos such as sex and death, the state of our personal finances remains a forbidden topic. Oh, you're free to discuss the performance of your stock portfolio, but don't dare pass judgment on someone else's spending habits. This credo, by which we take it on faith that what we do with our money is no one's business but our own, is the final triumph of *laissez faire* capitalism over the American soul.

Rudderless in a Tempestous Fiscal Sea

As a result of this lack of guidance, Christians have been left rudderless in a tempestuous fiscal sea. One study conducted by Princeton sociologist Robert Wuthnow deduced that Americans are spiritually adrift when it comes to making decisions about their personal finances. Though they continue to navigate with a vague awareness of the biblical warnings concerning the corrupting power of money, their sense of rectitude is hazy at best. Where once the church felt no compulsion against offering its parishioners practical advice for worldly living, Wuthnow argues it has since lost its social bite. Instead the church has become a cuddly agent of psychological well-being, an undemanding source of unconditional support. Consequently, Wuthnow concludes, the faithful end up living their economic lives "pretty much the same as those who have no faith at all."

In *Abundance: Living Responsibly With God's Gifts* we'll breach the wall of silence surrounding money. During the course of our Bible study, we'll wrestle with our personal finances, seeking always to discern the will of God. Fortunately, if we will only have ears to hear, we are blessed with an abundant biblical guidance. For Jesus really did have a preoccupation with wealth, speaking of money five times as often as prayer. Of course, his interest in wealth was not in its pursuit, but in the danger it posed to Christian discipleship. "It is easier for a camel to go through the eye of a needle," he said, "than for someone who is rich to enter the kingdom of God." Shocked, his disciples asked, "Then who can be saved?" Jesus replied, "For mortals it is impossible, but for God all things are possible" (Matthew 19:24-26). Together we will discover the promise of new life imbedded in his words.

THAT YOU MAY HAVE ABUNDANT LIFE

> This session is designed to introduce and define *abundance*.

GETTING STARTED

Kumiko: Kumiko was a woman striving to reach the top in a profession dominated by men: medicine. She had worked hard to accomplish her dream of becoming a doctor, yet as a member of a minority group, she felt she couldn't let up on herself. It seemed as if whenever she reached a goal she had set for herself, the bar would suddenly be raised. Always pushing to compete with her male colleagues, Kumiko believed that her work consumed her waking hours. Exhausted, with zero time or energy for relationships, she felt like a hamster on a wheel, frantically spinning but going nowhere. Sometimes, before collapsing into bed for a few hours sleep, Kumiko caught herself wondering, *"Is this all?"*

Welcome the group members. Introduce yourselves by sharing your name and a memory of the first time you had money of your own. What did you spend it on? Did you save any? Do you remember having a piggy bank? Did you receive an allowance?

Money is a sensitive topic for many people. Covenant with each other that during the next seven weeks no one will be forced to reveal more about their personal finances than they wish. Nor will group members share the personal financial information of others outside of class. This pledge of confidentiality is essential if trust is to exist within the group. However, having said that, there may be times when our financial values and practices are challenged by the gospel and other group members. After all, we are here to wrestle with what abundance means and the role wealth plays in our life and to discover anew the transforming power of Christ.

Carl: Carl had finally come to a realization: He hated his job. Although he was a budding artist in high school, his parents had convinced him art was a dead end. Instead, Carl majored in information technology in college, eventually landing a lucrative position with a Seattle software giant. After five years chained to his computer station, he'd begun to amass the rewards of the information revolution: a palatial home on Lake Washington, a membership to an exclusive athletic club, and a high-end "Beamer." Yet, despite the accouterments of success, Carl felt a vague sense of dissatisfaction. *"Is this going to be my life?"* he'd ask himself. *"Am I working like a slave 80 hours a week so that I can retire at 45—rich and alone?"* Increasingly, Carl found himself staring at his computer screen, wondering, *"Is this all?"*

Malcolm: During the seven years Malcolm had been out of college, he had worked for a national organization dedicated to the creation of affordable inner city housing. He had received a small monetary stipend, which, since he was living communally with others, satisfied his material needs. The simplicity of his lifestyle was more than made up for by his passion for the cause.

Disillusionment set in the day it was discovered that the nonprofit's key leader had been embezzling funds. Eventually Malcolm left to join the "9–5" crowd, becoming a moderately successful insurance salesman. Like many people consumed by their job, his marriage fell apart, leaving him $100,000 in debt. He found himself longing for the past, when a sense of purpose had energized his life. Some days, as Malcolm sat in his office working on claim forms, he'd catch himself pondering, *"Is this all?"*

THE ABUNDANT LIFE

Young adulthood is a time of searching. No longer under the protective wing of parents, our 20s and 30s are spent establishing a sense of independent selfhood. It is a time of questioning, a time of making choices that will effect our lives for decades to come: Where should I live? Should I go to college? enter the military? the Peace Corps? Should I get married? start a family?

Many of the choices confronting us concern money, the topic of this Bible study: Should I begin a career? What occupation should I enter? What training will I need? How much money do I require? How will I spend my money?

In short, we must answer the question: What is "the good life?" Or to phrase the question biblically, "What is the abundant life?" It is a question fraught with tension between two potentially competing deities: God and wealth, or what the Bible sometimes calls "mammon" (Matthew 6:24). Whichever we choose, it will serve as our guiding template for life.

What Is Abundance?

We begin our effort to define "the abundant life" by looking up the word *abundant* in a dictionary. The tension inherent in any attempt to define "the abundant life" is clear the moment we begin to read. According to Webster, the first meaning is "very plentiful; more than sufficient; ample." The synonym that comes to mind is "satisfaction." But the second meaning of the word *abundant* is "well-supplied; rich (in something)," a meaning that indicates "excess."

Therein lies the rub and the source of a great deal of the confusion surrounding the

The Abundant Life
Read Matthew 6:24. What does this say about the clash between God and wealth? Do you agree?

What Is Abundance?
How would you define *abundance*.
How can it imply both "sufficient" and "excess"? What, do you think, are gradations on the sliding scale of abundance?

concept of the abundant life. According to the first definition, *abundant* is synonymous with "ample" ("enough to fill the needs; adequate"). Yet according to the second, the word *abundant* means "to be rich in something," ("having more than enough of material possessions"). Thus *abundant* seems to contain a sliding scale of meaning: from "adequate" to "having more than enough." In other words, as in life, the definition of *abundant* changes depending on the perspective we choose.

Material Possessions

The predominant societal understanding of the abundant or good life is rooted in personal achievement, which in turn, is measured by our material possessions. According to this definition, one's personal worth is equivalent to one's social standing, which is usually commensurate to the amount of wealth one has accumulated. Perhaps the ubiquitous bumper sticker says it best: "The one who dies with the most toys wins." Thus, an endless quest to secure more dominates our waking hours. Our life becomes one of striving, our feelings of inadequacy fueled by a constant barrage of advertisements, without whose products, we are told, acceptance and love are impossible.

Researchers have documented the growing influence of this "toys" approach to fulfillment. In 1967, UCLA began polling incoming freshmen, asking them a series of questions intended to reveal their values. In the initial year of the survey, a majority (82 percent) of the students said it was extremely important to "develop a meaningful philosophy of life." By 1997, thirty years later, the goal of "developing a meaningful philosophy of life" had dropped to sixth place. In its stead, "being well-off financially" had

DISCUSS

Material Possessions
Are we becoming more materialistic as a society? Are our children becoming more materialistic? (Refer to the UCLA poll of incoming freshmen.) What forces in society are driving our current level of materialism? What role does advertising play? peer pressure? How do you feel about having the most or best "toys"?

become the primary concern of the majority (74 percent) of the students. Score one for mammon.

I Need "I Want"

The pitfall inherent within our society's tendency to measure self-worth in silver and gold, as Jesus well knew, was that, as an approach to life, it leads inevitably to anxiety. For it is human nature to never be satisfied with what we have. Just when we've reached the point that we can finally say "enough," another bauble appears enticingly on the horizon. What is a luxury one day is transformed into a necessity the next.

For proof, we need look no farther than our own living room. According to the Roper Center survey, only ten percent of their 1975 respondents thought a second color television part of "the good life." By 1991 however, the number who thought a second television was a necessary accouterment to their lifestyle had risen to 28 percent. This increase in perceived need was reflected in every category—from owning a second car to a vacation home.

The Satisfaction Quotient

Nor has our accumulation of "stuff" made us any happier than our parents were at our age. Just think of all the technological marvels we rely upon today that were unavailable a generation ago. In 1958, only four percent of American homes enjoyed the convenience of a dishwasher. Today more than half do. Likewise, in 1958, less than one percent of American households had a color television; now 97 percent have one. Yet, at the same time, the increase of "baubles" has not triggered a corresponding upsurge in personal satisfaction.

I Need "I Want"
Brainstorm a list of all the things you have that you feel you just can't get along without. Then work out a simple ranking system to quantify the level of actual need that the item fulfills (for example, a 5 for the absolute "really need" item and 1 for the "I want but don't have to have" item).

Rank your own list of stuff and compare it with the rankings of others. How much of "I need" is really closer to "I want"?

Satisfaction Quotient
Think about the lyrics of music you hear, whether it's from pop, jazz, rap, swing, hymns, or other, that have to do with possessions or abundance in any form. What do these lyrics celebrate, in terms of possessions or abundance? yearn for? criticize? (Sing your answer if you wish!)

SMALL
GROUP

Form two teams. One team will debate the merits of "the good life" as understood from their parents' or grandparents' generation, and the other team will debate the issue from a current understanding. ("The good life" can include both tangible and intangible examples of what brings happiness or satisfaction to life.)

What are the differences in perspective? What has been gained or lost through the years? What effect does this have on your perspective? your orientation to abundance?

How do we know? Well, believe it or not, there are people who are paid to measure our general level of contentment. According to the *American Demographics* "Index of Well-Being," happiness has not kept pace with our economic fortune. Richard A. Easterlin, an economist at the University of Southern California, points out that the steady growth in the American economy has not been accompanied by an increase in people's self-assessment of their own happiness. "There has been no improvement in average happiness in the United States over almost a half century," he said, "a period in which real gross domestic product per capita more than doubled. Even though each generation has more income than its predecessor, each generation also wants more than its predecessor."

Thus, for those who adopt society's formulation of "the good life," that abundance equals the accumulation of wealth, anxiety is a constant companion. Those who feel they don't have enough, fret over their ability to gain more. And those who already have much, worry about maintaining and protecting their stash. In the end, no one wins.

PRESCRIPTION FOR ANXIETY

Whereas society presents us a vision of "the good life" resplendent with "toys," Jesus offers a much different understanding of the "abundant life"; one not based upon a disparity of wealth, but upon the kingdom of God in which everyone shares in the Lord's abundance. Upon the advent of his ministry, Jesus opened the Isaiah scroll and read: "The Spirit of the Lord is upon me, / because he has anointed me / to bring good news to the poor. / He has sent me to proclaim release to the captives / and recovery of sight to the blind, / to let the oppressed go free, / to proclaim the year of the Lord's favor" (Luke 4:18-19; see Isaiah 61:1-2).

Thus Jesus, from the very beginning of his mission, equates the coming of the kingdom of God with the deliverance of the impoverished and the oppressed. The image he uses is that of "the year of the Lord's favor," a reference to the Jubilee year described in Leviticus 25, a time of economic restoration when all debts were forgiven, the poor restored to the land, and selfish individualism put to death.

BIBLE

Rx for Anxiety
Divide Luke 4:18-19; 12:22-34; and Galatians 5:22-26 among three small groups. What is Jesus' prescription for anxiety? What is the relationship between anxiety and the "fruits of the Spirit?" How many of the "fruits of the Spirit" are evidenced in your own life? Are you troubled by anxiety? What is making you anxious? Our economy is humming along and many of us have more "toys" than ever—why then are we increasingly anxious?

Biblical Studies 101: Jubilee

In Leviticus 25, the Isrealites were commanded by Yahweh to observe a sabbatical for the land and its inhabitants every fifty years. The Jubilee year was to be a year of rest. The Israelites were entitled to eat the food that grew in the fallow fields, but they were not to raise crops for profit.

Likewise, all land that had been confiscated for the repayment of debts was to be returned to the original owner. Slaves were to be emancipated and personal debt forgiven. In so doing, the Hebrews acknowledged their own indebtedness to Yahweh.

Deuteronomy 15:1-2 calls for a sabbatical every seventh year. It reads: "Every seventh year you shall grant a remission of debts. And this is the manner of the remission: every creditor shall remit the claim that is held against a neighbor, not exacting it of a neighbor who is a member of the community, because the LORD's remission has been proclaimed." Apparently the forgiveness of debts was applicable to a member of one's own community, but not to a foreigner.

Jesus observed no such restriction in his own teaching. In Luke 4, he appropriates the vision of the Jubilee found in Isaiah 61, promising "release to the captives." As his actions would later make clear, Jesus did not exclude persons from the benefits of Jubilee. Instead, he proclaimed the good news of the coming kingdom to Israelite and foreigner alike.

Jubilee

Review Leviticus 25 and Deuteronomy 15. Use a Bible dictionary for more information. Discuss the Jubilee. What was the purpose of the Jubilee? Was it ever enacted in ancient Israel? What would be the results if such a program were ever instituted in the United States? Would our economy collapse if personal debt was suddenly forgiven? How might we practice some form of Jubilee in our country? in our church? in our personal lives?

LOOK CLOSER

Read John 10:1-10. Ask group members to describe the pastoral image Jesus employed. Who is the shepherd? Who are the sheep? Is it possible for the sheep to survive without the shepherd? What is Jesus saying about Christian community? Is the abundant life lived in isolation? What is the end result of our "finding pasture" with Christ?

Create a fence with a gate from construction paper. After fastening it to the wall of your room, have group members each cut out a shape of a sheep (this doesn't have to be perfect!), write his or her name on it, and place it inside the fence. Throughout the following weeks of study it will serve as a visual reminder of your Christian community.

In keeping with the Jubilee's image of agricultural bounty, the Apostle Paul describes the harvest of the kingdom of God as the fruits of the Spirit: "love, joy, peace, patience, kindness, generosity, faithfulness, gentleness, and self-control" (Galatians 5:22-26). The spirit of greed and anxiety ("the flesh with its passions and desires") has been crucified. No longer are envy, conceit, and competition the laws that govern our relationship with each other. Instead, Christians live in and are guided by the Spirit of the Lord. Score one for God.

Close with this prayer: "Gracious God, we thank you for your offer of abundant life. Grant us the wisdom and the courage to live financially as your disciples. May our lives proclaim the overwhelming joy of the kingdom of God and witness to the fact that the best things in life truly are free. Be with this group during the coming weeks. Bind us together in your love. We pray this in the name of Jesus, who is the Christ. Amen."

A LAND "FLOWING WITH MILK AND HONEY"

This session will examine biblical passages about God's tangible blessings and how we might interpret the idea of material wealth today.

SETTING STARTED

God desires abundant life for us. In the last session, we discussed New Testament images of abundance. The Hebrew Scriptures also contain many passages cataloging God's desire for us to enjoy a full and plentiful existence. Within the first chapter of Genesis, God declares the divine handiwork good no less than seven times. It is a picture of a lush, verdant world bursting with abundance. "See," said God to humankind, "I have given you every plant yielding seed that is upon the face of all the earth, and every tree with seed in its fruit, you shall have them for food" (Genesis 1: 29).

God's Tangible Blessings

The second creation story (Genesis 2:4b-25) is resplendent with images of abundance, as well. Having created the man, Adam, Yahweh planted "a garden in Eden," a paradise boasting of "every tree that is pleasant to the sight and good for food" (2:9). God sweetened the pot even further by creating woman, whom the man named Eve. And there we might have stayed, enjoying a garden party that would have made even Martha Stewart envious. Instead, Adam and

Do a quick update on how group members are doing. Introduce any new participants.

God's Blessings
Read Genesis 1–2, the two Creation stories. The first is rich in majesty and reveals the creative initiative of a powerful God. The second is probably an earlier story; a warm, personal account that describes the relationship of the man and woman to God, to each other, and to the rest of Creation. What was God's intention in Creation? What was the nature of God's blessing upon Creation?

Eve broke their covenant with God, eating of the tree of knowledge. Their consumption of the forbidden fruit was an attempt to cast aside our dependence on God, to become instead "like God" ourselves, and because of it, humankind was driven from Eden.

East of Eden

East of Eden
Read Genesis 3–4.
What was the sin that provoked God (Yahweh) to drive Adam and Eve out of the garden of Eden? What was life like for them east of Eden? Why did Cain and Abel return a portion of their bounty to God? After the Fall (the sin and banishment from the garden), how would you describe the nature of God's blessing on the woman and man? on the rest of Creation?

Read the rest of the Scriptures that describe the blessings of wealth on the patriarchs (Abraham, Isaac, Jacob) and Solomon. Did God's blessing always imply that the blessed would be wealthy? That the wealthy were wealthy because they were blessed?

Yet despite their sin of self-aggrandizement, God did not abandon Adam and Eve. Instead, Yahweh's desire for an abundant life for all creation survived their betrayal. Though humankind was not allowed to re-enter Paradise, God's beneficence continued to flow, even east of Eden. Adam and Eve were blessed with two sons: Cain, described as a "tiller of the ground" (4:2), and Abel, a "keeper of sheep." Each prospered, eventually returning to God a portion of their bounty. This first offering was given in recognition that all wealth comes from God.

For Christians steeped in the New Testament, it is tempting to spiritualize the gifts of God. But the writers of Israel's sacred texts would have none of it. Just as it was God's pleasure to gift humankind with the garden, so too would God bestow upon Israel a promised land flowing with "milk and honey." These were not ethereal blessings but earthly delights.

The ancient Hebrews also understood that if Yahweh could gift an entire people, so too could God bless individuals with material wealth. In the case of Abraham, God promised to make of him "a great nation" (Genesis 12:2), a pledge that included "livestock, silver, and gold" (13:2). Likewise it was said of Abraham's son Isaac, "The LORD blessed him, and the man became rich" (26:12-13). Even Jacob, who secured his father's blessing through deceit, could afford to offer his brother Esau a fortune in compensation (32:13-21). Yahweh also rewarded Solomon with "riches" (1 Kings 3:13). Thus it was accepted that material possessions were in keeping with, and indeed evidence of, God's blessing.

JUSTICE FOR THE "HAVE-NOTS"

But God's blessing came with strings attached. Wealth carried an ethical caveat to care for the poor. Israelites were not free to spend their wealth as they pleased, without regard for their community. After all, the land on which they had prospered belonged not to them but to God. In return, Israel's bounty was to be shared. This injunction included widows, orphans, Levites, and the sojourner; each of whom were cut off from the land, the source of Israel's wealth. For example, the Lord appeared to Abraham in the guise of three strangers (Genesis 18:1-15). In response, Abraham provided an elaborate meal, an expected act of hospitality.

In Deuteronomy 15:11, Moses admonished Israel to care for the poor. "I therefore command you," he said, speaking for God, " 'Open your hand to the poor and the needy neighbor in your land.' " Thus, from the beginning of Israel's foundation, the love of God was associated with loving one's neighbor.

Given human nature, we are more often made aware of this scriptural covenant on behalf of the poor by its transgression, rather than by its fulfillment. The call for justice is a dominant theme throughout the Hebrew text, especially among the prophets. The wealthy are often castigated for their apathy towards the less fortunate. Illustrative of the righteous anger of the

Read Exodus 3:7-12; 33:1-6; Leviticus 20:22-26; Numbers 13:21-24; Deuteronomy 6:1-15; and 8:1-20. Describe the Promised Land. From the perspective of the Israelites wandering in the wilderness, what would have been "milk and honey?" How does our society define "milk and honey?" How do you define "milk and honey" in your life? Does "milk and honey" come directly from God or through our own effort?

Justice
In Genesis 18, Abraham models the hospitality that God demands Israel show the outcast and sojourner. How is your church practicing hospitality to the stranger? How are you personally exhibiting hospitality in your life?

Use a Bible dictionary to look up *hospitality*. How is the practice of hospitality an act of blessing? How is hospitality practiced in your culture and how is it alike or dissimilar to biblical hospitality? What lessons about abundance and blessing can we learn from the practice of biblical hospitality?

Form two or three small groups and look at the passage from Jeremiah. How would you paraphrase it? Think of a new way to present the message: a poem, rap, jingle, limerick, or other paraphrase and present it to the other groups. What is the message about abundance that transcends time and culture?

prophets is the Book of Jeremiah. On behalf of God, Jeremiah decries injustice, saying: "For scoundrels are found among my people; / they take over the goods of others. / Like fowlers they set a trap; / they catch human beings. / Like a cage full of birds, / their houses are full of treachery; / therefore they have become great and rich, / they have grown fat and sleek. / They know no limits in deeds of wickedness; / they do not judge with justice / the cause of the orphan, to make it prosper, / and they do not defend the rights of the needy" (5:26-28).

Jeremiah later exhorted the king of Judah to "act with justice and righteousness, and deliver from the hand of the oppressor anyone who has been robbed. And do no wrong or violence to the alien, the orphan, and the widow" (22:3). Notice the issue at hand is not wealth, but its distribution. While the biblical writers may have believed money to be a partner in evil, it was not inherently evil in and of itself. Rather the prophets railed against the rich because they had ignored their responsibility toward "the least of these."

Dire Consequences

BIBLE

Dire Consequences
Read the following passages: Isaiah 58:1-14; Jeremiah 21:1-10; 22:3-5; Amos 5:10-13, 18-24. Why did the prophets demand justice for the needy? What were the consequences of disobedience? What is the relationship of abundance to obedience? If one of the prophets was to peruse your check register, what do you think he'd say to you?

The consequences were grave. Having broken their covenant with God by trampling the poor, Yahweh withdrew protection, allowing Israel to be conquered. Jeremiah even goes so far as to describe King Nebuchadnezzar of Babylon as the instrument of God's punishment (21:1-10). The kingdom of Judah would be sacked, Jerusalem burned, the people taken into exile; and all the while, God would fight on behalf of the invaders. And when all Jeremiah had prophesied came to pass, and the citizens of Jerusalem were being taken into exile, some of the people "who owned nothing" stayed behind with "vineyards and fields" (39:10). Where once the rich had held sway, only the poor remained to enjoy the "milk and honey" of the Promised Land.

TIME TRAVEL

Ancient history? Let's fast forward 3,000 years. The United States is arguably the richest country in the world, a promised land flowing with "milk and honey." For much of the latter half of the 20th century, Americans have been the recipients of an unparalleled explosion of wealth. During the past 15 years there have been more billionaires created than at any other time of our fiscal history. But the real growth has come in the number of millionaires. In 1996, nearly five million American households had a net worth of over a million dollars, an increase of 118 percent since 1992. In turn, their bonanza raised the median net worth of the average American family.

Sean

"For someone who comes from a generation of 'slackers,' I'm doing pretty well. I've been told I'm in a generation of unfocused, go-nowhere X'ers; the first in US history that will be less well off than their parents. Well, guess what. I'm 28, I have a good education, a job that I like, and I'm closing on my own house in a couple of weeks. My dad can't claim that he did so well so quickly!"

Economic Disparity

Yet while America's wealth has skyrocketed, so has the economic disparity existing between its citizens. In 1979, the average household income of the top five percent was more than 10 times the bottom 20 percent. By 1989, the discrepancy had risen to nearly

Time Travel
Discuss the changes in the economy during the latter half of the 20th century that have allowed for the amassment of fortunes such as Bill Gates'.

Do you begrudge them their billions? Is it a sin to have so much when the majority of the world's population has so little? In other words, is it a sin to own a Lexus when children are dying of hunger? Does the fact that the super-wealthy donate a portion of their fortune to worthy causes entitle them to a clear conscience? Did you personally benefit from the "go-go" economy of the 1980's and 1990's? How have you given back?

Use Sean's example or one of your own to examine where you think you are in terms of having what you need, what you want, what you think you need, and how you use it. What is your sense of abundance? your sense of entitlement or access to certain possessions or opportunities? What role does your faith play in making this assessment?

16 to 1. And in 1999, it stood at 19 to 1, the largest divide since the Census Bureau started keeping these statistics in 1947. It is also, with 1 percent of the population holding 40 percent of the wealth (up from 19 percent from 1976), the largest economic disparity existing in the developed world.

Economists point to various reasons for the growing divide. The globalization of the economy in the 1980's forced American business to slash its work force in order to compete overseas. Down-sizing became a household word as thousands of lower- and middle-income manufacturing jobs were

Look Closer: The Bishops' Assessment

In 1996, ten years after they published their pastoral letter on the US economy, "Economic Justice for All," the Roman Catholic bishops of the United States revisited their conclusions. "We live in an economy of paradoxes," they wrote. "Profits, productivity, and the stock market have grown, while many workers' income and sense of security declined. Our economy is among the most powerful and productive on earth. But it is pulling us apart. We are one nation, but three economies."

The three economies they describe include the prosperous, productive economy fueled by the global marketplace and information age; the economy of those left behind—without jobs, fathers, or a living wage; and the shrinking, and increasingly anxious middle, wondering what it will take to push them over the edge. The bishops concluded, "We are still haunted by how the 'least among us' are faring. By this measure, our society is seriously failing."

lost. During the 1990's, white collar management discovered it too was vulnerable. The computer revolution swept over the economic landscape, creating what came to be called the "digital divide" between those with access to information technology and those without. The result has been that the true net wealth of the typical American household (minus the top 20 percent) has actually declined during the last decade.

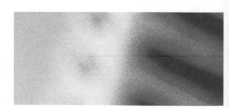

Chrystal and Perry

When is someone going to let us in on this prosperity kick? We both teach in elementary schools. It only takes a few kids who get no nurture or discipline at home to disrupt the entire class, and we get blamed for their poor performance. It's a wonder anyone can learn in that environment. And for being disciplinarian, "truancy police," surrogate parent, referee, and then teacher, we get a joint salary that barely pays the bills. For a household with two master's degrees, and two full-time jobs, we're going nowhere.

⅏Y SHARE OF THE GOODS

According to a 1998 study conducted by *Insight on the News* magazine, the average income of the poorest one-fifth of all families with children has fallen by one-fifth since the late 1970's; an average of $2,500 per family. On the other hand, the income of the top one-fifth of American households has risen an average of 30 percent, or $27,000. At the same time, the wages of middle-income families have remained stagnant. Rather than having entered the economic promised land, many employees are in fact working more hours for less income.

Another factor in America's economic disparity is the bullish stock market. Media reports of overnight internet moguls aside, relatively few Americans have benefited from the surge in stock prices, although more seem to have access than ever before. According to the Federal Reserve Board's 1995 "Survey of Consumer Finances," of the 40 percent of American households with

CASE STUDY Use Chrystal and Perry's situation or one of your own to examine how you feel to be left out of the abundance parade. Would you stay away from a "noble profession" if it were not also lucrative, or at least financially comfortable? How do you define *abundance* in terms of your work and what you perceive as its rewards?

SMALL GROUP

My Share
Form small groups. All group members will write their own money autobiography individually. Consider these issues for the autobiography: the place money held in your childhood; your parents' or guardians' attitude towards money; how the family's income was shared with you; whether you grew up feeling deprived or privileged; how these influences shape your relationship with money today.

When the autobiography is done, discuss them with the other small group members. How has your attitude changed toward money over the years? What has influenced any changes? Have the changes been positive or negative? What are your feelings towards money? Is money equal in your mind to security? Do you ever feel guilty about your spending? What does your faith have to do with your attitude toward and your decisions about money?

market investments, 72 percent had holdings worth less than $5,000.

One critic summed up the situation this way: "Plato told Aristotle that no one should have more than five times the wealth of the lowest-paid member of society. The ratios of today would totally blow Plato away. Last year, the pay of a big-company chief executive was 350 times that of the average worker. In 2010, the gap is projected to be that between Louis XVI and his workers—and you know what happened to Louis XVI."

BACK TO GOD'S BLESSING

Is Sean especially blessed by God, but not Chrystal and Perry? Is the Bible a "prosperity gospel" that implicitly condemns those who don't have as somehow undeserving, lazy, or otherwise to blame for their lack of material things? Or must we go back to the dark days when the man and woman were expelled from Eden—the beginning of sin—to understand why there is inequity and want in this life?

While there is biblical testimony that we shall always have the poor with us, it is not God's will that some should be in want, especially while others prosper. Louis XVI may have lost his head, but God wants us to keep our heads—and our body and soul together. After all, God created them to be good.

Back to Blessing
Consider the questions posed in the text. What would you say now to Sean and Chrystal and Perry?

What role does sin have in the relationship between abundance and want? between blessing and "expulsion from economic Eden"?

Close with a prayer for all those who are struggling both with want and with greed. Pray for God's economic justice and hospitality for all.

THE OVER-INDULGED LIFE

This session is designed to examine need, want, and the symptoms and consequences of "affluenza."

GETTING STARTED

Abundance and wealth are relative terms, we think. To the fabulously wealthy, it's not worth the time to pick up $500 from the street. Most of the rest of the world would love to know where this street is! That $500 could be a month's rent or two years' income.

Exchange your gestures of welcome and introduce anyone new to the study.

Ask: How would you define *wealth*? Is there some specific amount or ratio that for you is the threshold between comfortable and affluent or well-off and between well-off and wealthy?

MATERIAL WORLD

"What is the abundant life?" In 1993, Peter Menzel set out to find the answer by photographing 30 families from across the world and their household possessions. The result was *Material World: a Global Family Portrait* (Sierra Club Books, San Francisco, 1994). *Material World* is a fascinating snapshot of the world in the last decade of the 20th century. It is both thought-provoking and, when read from the perspective of the developed world, disturbing. The contrast between the First and Third World is striking, especially when images of poverty and prosperity are placed in juxtaposition, as on the front cover.

Material World
List your household possessions on a sheet of paper or draw a simple picture in the style of the book *Material World*.

If you can obtain a copy at your local library, look through some of the photographs. What influence does seeing the juxtaposition of affluence and wealth have on you? Do any of the photos remind you of anything in your family's situation or history? Explain.

SMALL GROUP

Form groups of three or four persons. Imagine that you share a house, which has caught fire. Among you, you can only save one or two items. What would it be? How would you decide? Why is this particular object so precious? Thinking only of your own possessions, have any of your belongings remained unused over the past year? Do you think you have too much stuff? not enough? or just right?

DISCUSS

Compare the amount of material possessions we own compared to the Namgay family of Bhutan. Is it an injustice that we have so much more? Why are some people poor and others rich in this world? Is that how God wants it?

The top of the page is a portrait of the Skeens of Texas. They were judged a typical American family and, from our point of view, there's nothing exceptional about the array of possessions set out in their front yard. After all, most of us probably own a similar collection of material possessions.

Neither does the family's image seem unusual. Rick and Patty are posed with their two children. Rick stands solemnly, his cowboy hat held over his heart. Beside him, Julie holds their most prized possession: the Holy Bible.

Directly beneath the picture of the Skeens is a portrait of the Namgay family of Bhutan. Life is obviously a struggle. The father, at 50 years of age, is on borrowed time. In his country, male life expectancy is 47 years. According to Bhutan actuarial tables, his wife, who is 47, can herself expect only two more years of life. Given the deep creases that line their faces, each could be mistaken for 70. Their possessions consist of hoes, baskets, a clay pot, blankets, a butter churn, a wooden yoke and a few animals. Namgay, his wife, and their three children are kneeling behind a family altar, in the middle of which stands a small golden statue. It is Namtose, the Buddhist god of wealth.

MANNA

Compared to the wilderness in which Israel wandered, Bhutan is the garden of Eden. Staggered by a lack of food and water, the Israelites complained bitterly, chastising Moses for taking them from the "fleshpots" of slavery. In response, Yahweh provided richly for the people's needs. In Exodus 16:1-21, manna and quail were sent to stem their hunger. Hosea interprets this initial wilderness period as an innocent time of courtship between God and Israel (Hosea 2:14-15).

GRAVES OF CRAVING

However, following the covenant at Mount Sinai, the honeymoon was over. Murmuring became equated with rebellion. Israel's complaints were no longer greeted with equanimity but judgment. In Numbers 11:1-15, 31-35, the people's complaints finally kindled the Lord's anger (11:1). As earlier, quail were provided, but when the "rabble among them" (11:4) began to eat, Yahweh struck them down "while the meat was still between their teeth" (11:33). This was a warning to the remaining Israelites that the rules had changed; a warning immortalized in the name of the rabble's burial site: the "Graves of Craving."

INDIGESTION

Ancient history? Again we fast forward 3,000 years. Americans, by feeding an insatiable hunger for material goods, may be digging their own "graves of craving." At the very least, our rich diet threatens us with a major case of indigestion. For clearly we are wallowing in a glut of "stuff," the result of history's greatest buying binge. While the economic disparity between rich and poor remains worrisome, the general economic welfare of many Americans has risen steadily.

The fact is that all but the very poorest of the poor in our society live better than the majority of Americans a century ago. And

Manna
In pairs, read Exodus 16:1-21. What was Israel's response to life in the wilderness? Why did they long to return to Egypt? What was God's response to the complaints of the first generation? What happened when some of the people attempted to hoard their "daily bread?"

Graves of Craving
Read Numbers 11:1-15, 31-35. How does this feeding in the wilderness compare to the previous one in Exodus 16:1-21? How much quail did they gather? Why was the Lord's anger kindled? What is the significance of the phrase "while the meat was still between their teeth"? (None were allowed to satisfy their hunger.) Why was the burial site named the "graves of craving?"

Indigestion
In small groups, draw a diagram of your childhood home and of your current residence. Show your artwork and discuss with each other how they compare. Has your family's level of consumption risen during the past decade? How?

Re-examine your list of material possessions. Rate each possession as "luxury," "convenience," or "necessity." Explain your designation. Would you have ranked any of the items differently five or ten years ago? What belongings do you possess that were not available to your parents at your age? Are you better or worst off financially than your parents? Do you and your parents have any disagreements concerning money and material possessions and how to handle them? Do you think Americans are more materialistic now than in the past? Are we digging our own "graves of craving?"

Juanito

Use the comments by Juanito to discuss issues of consumption or propose a case from your own experience. What are Juanito's issues? his perspective on things? his priorities? Does his story sound real to you? Does it match your own experience? Explain. How might his culture influence his thinking on this issue? What can it teach someone from another culture?

the pace of acquisition is accelerating. As of 1970, the living space of the typical American household has nearly doubled; the number of families who own two or more vehicles has risen from 29 percent to 62 percent; and air travel has quadrupled. Personal services, such as household cleaning and private childcare, have also risen perceptively, as has the demand for luxury goods. According to the *Atlantic Monthly*, (June, 1999) since 1993, general consumption has risen 29 percent; expensive adventure travel is up 46 percent; sales of gourmet chocolates up 51 percent, pearls 73 percent, and luxury cars 74 percent. Even yacht sales, the quintessential symbol of success, has shot up 143 percent.

All this conspicuous consumption begs the question: Just because we can have it, do we really need it?" In her book, *Simplify Your Life*, author Elaine St. James poses the question this way: "How has it happened that the size of the average American home has gone from the roughly 900-square-foot, two-bedroom, one-bath home of the 1950's to a roughly 2,000-square-foot home with three bedrooms, three and a half baths, an eat-in kitchen, a dining room, a library, an exercise room, a 'great' room, a TV room, at least a two- but often a three-car garage, and an entry hall that rivals the size of the Sistine Chapel? It certainly did not happen because of the need to house larger families; the average family size has gone from four in the 1950's to 2.5 in the 1990's."

Juanito

I'm Puerto Rican, from La Perla near the capital of San Juan. Everyone has a beautiful view of the ocean; our community is right at the water. It's also one of the poorest places there. I moved to New York to get a good job, and I did. I've started at the bottom, but when I told my mother about it, she started to cry—for joy. Even my modest salary is three times what my father ever earned in a year. I know what it's like to want and not have, and it's tempting to go after it all now. But first things first; I'm going to help my family.

AFFLUENZA

There is another question beyond "Do we need it?" and that is, "Is all this stuff really good for us?" The popular PBS production "Affluenza" reports that in the past two decades, as our per capita consumption has risen 45 percent, our quality of life (as measured by the Index of Social Health) has gone down 52 percent. Host Scott Simon attributes the decline to "affluenza," a "disease" whose symptoms include "a feeling of perpetual disappointment with our lives and ... an insatiable desire for material goods."

Are we infected? Is America's vision of "the good life" literally making us sick? Let's consider some of the possible warning signs:

Less Leisure Time

First, we have less leisure time. In order to afford all our stuff, Americans are working more than ever. Only a generation ago, experts were predicting modern technology would make possible a 15-hour work week by the year 2000. Instead, despite the promised increase in productivity, Americans are laboring 15 percent more now than they did in 1973. *USA Today* (March, 1997) reports that, compared to

Do you agree with the quality of life finding of the Index of Social Health? What factors might the Index be using to quantify "quality of life?"

Look at the symptoms of affluenza. Are you infected? Other family members, including your children? What are the causes of affluenza? What role does advertising and the entertainment industry play in the spread of affluenza? (Consider taking the affluenza test found at the following Internet address: *http://www.pbs.org/kcts/affluenza/diag/what.html*)

SMALL GROUP

Form three groups to consider the information in "Less Leisure Time," "Strung Out," and "Greed." Discuss the impact of affluenza on the topic assigned to the group using these questions.

Less Leisure

Do you have time to do the things you most like to do? What gets in the way of doing the things you most want to do? Do you agree that Americans are working more now than in the past? What impact has technology had upon your work? upon your leisure time? How much time do you spend together as a family? Are both you and your spouse working? How has that affected your family life? How many days of paid vacation do you receive a year? (In Europe, four weeks of paid vacation a year is mandatory and six weeks customary.) When was the last time your family took an extended vacation? Are Americans shortchanging themselves on their leisure time? What does your faith suggest to you about the value of leisure time?

Look up these biblical passages about sabbath: Genesis 2:2-3; Exodus 20:8; Jeremiah 17:21-27; Mathew 12:12; Mark 2:27. How is sabbath linked with leisure time? What is the difference? With these biblical injunctions in mind, what insight do you gain into the stresses of daily life?

Strung Out

Do you ever feel stressed because you don't have enough time? Do you worry about how you're going to pay your bills? How has the "work-spend" treadmill affected your life and those of your loved ones? Can you relate to the statement, "I have no life." Do you feel your life is out of balance?

1969, today's employees spend an additional 160 hours a year on the job.

The result of this trend is less time spent together as families. Today's parents spend 40 percent less time with their children than those of a generation ago. According to the "Affluenza" website (*www.pbs.org/kcts/affluenza*) working couples spend 40 minutes a week playing with their children, and slightly more (12 minutes a day) interacting with each other. "North Americans have to work more in order to buy things," observes Inez de Rake of Bolivia. "For that reason they spend less time with their families, thinking that to be comfortable is more important for the family than to give them love and time together."

Strung Out

In addition to lost family time, all those hours on the job create stress, the second symptom of affluenza. Increasingly, American workers feel like a hamster spinning its wheel. According to a recent Lou Harris poll, 86 percent of us complain of chronic stress. Another survey reveals many of us no longer experience stress as an "occasional crisis," but as a "continual state of existence." "We hear the same refrain all the time," says Gerald Celente, of the Trends Research Institute, a social analysis think tank in Rinebeck, New York. "I have no life.... I get home at night, there's laundry, bills to pay.... I'm exhausted, I go to sleep, I wake up and the routine begins the next day all over again."

Not long ago, elevated levels of stress in our lives were considered a harmless byproduct of modern life. But, today's medical researchers are not so sure. According to Dr. Paul Rosch, president of the American Institute of Stress, there is now significant evidence that stress is related to potentially life-threatening illnesses. The

Japanese even coined a term for lethal, work-induced stress: *karoshi*, which means literally "death from overwork."

Greed

The third consequence of affluenza is avarice. Researchers have, over the past few decades, tracked a gradual increase in the level of our material expectation. Items once considered luxuries, such as cars and color televisions, became conveniences, and eventually transformed to necessities. In other words, as our income rises, our aspirations do as well. Consequently, we continue to run faster and faster in order to stay in one place. The outlook for a simpler, less materialistic future is not too promising.

LINE IN THE SAND

Tina

I have spent most of my life in school. I started working full-time about a year and a half ago. You wouldn't believe the starting pay! I have a master's degree, and my salary is a mere $29,000. Still, it beats the hand-to-mouth life of a student. It feels great to finally buy the stuff that a young professional should have—nice furniture for my apartment, new CD player, dinner out to treat my friends—but you should hear my dad. To hear him talk, you'd think everyone should start at the bottom like he did. Not me; I'm young, I'm smart; I'm going to have it all.

Only One Master

In Session 2, we learned that the Hebrew Scriptures do not condemn money outright.

LOOK CLOSER

Read Matthew 6:25-34. What does this passage say to you about daily stresses and God's care? Is it naïve to think in today's business environment that trusting in God is sufficient? Explain. What does it mean to you personally that striving for the Kingdom will bring you whatever else you need (including righteousness)?

DISCUSS

Greed
Has the level of your material expectation risen over the past decade? Can you think of some possessions in your life that started as luxuries and gradually became necessities? Are you more materialistic than your parents? How attached are you to your belongings? If Jesus were to ask you to give what you have to the poor and follow him, would you? What is the lure of shopping and material possessions?

CASE STUDY

Tina
Use Tina's story to start a discussion on having it all or use a situation from your own experience. What is Tina's attitude about what she has? about what she *ought* to have? about her father's attitude and work ethic? What would you like to tell her about her attitude? about her spending habits? about the apparent disparity between her father's perceptions and her own?

Only One Master
Read Matthew 6:24. By comparing mammon to God, Jesus elevated money to the status of a rival god. Why is this significant? Do Americans worship money? In whom do you place your trust: God or mammon?

Read Mark 10:17-31. The story is open-ended; we don't know what the man did, except to leave in sadness. Suggest endings to the story either by having one person begin and add a few new sentences to the story, then another, then another, until the last group member concludes the incident; or by having each group member write his or her own ending. How do you feel about the new ending(s)? How do they square with "real life"? with a life of faith? Is there a difference? If so, why?

Why did Jesus tell the rich man to give away what he had to the poor? Does he expect that of each of us? What stands in your way to an intimate and trusting relationship with God? What might you be asked to give up? Why?

Pray that God will heal us of affluenza and empower us to use our resources in the service of others.

Instead, the text decries its misuse; recognizing the subversive danger it presents to Israel's covenant to God and neighbor. Jesus stood firmly in this tradition. He too realized wealth's tendency towards corruption. But he went even further in his condemnation of its ability to ensnare.

In Matthew 6:24, he says, "No one can serve two masters; for a slave will either hate the one and love the other, or be devoted to the one and despise the other. You cannot serve God and wealth." The Aramaic word he would have used for "wealth" is *mammon*. By contrasting mammon to God, he imbued it with the spiritual authority of a rival and idolatrous god. And as his Jewish listeners knew well, there could be only one God for Israel (Exodus 20:3). Only one loyalty. Only one choice.

Jesus' challenge to his audience was in keeping with his general teaching on greed. When he required the rich man to give away what he had (Mark 10:17-22), Jesus did so not because he thought money inherently evil. After all, he depended upon the generosity of others to support his mission (Luke 8:1-3). But Jesus realized the tremendous power wealth held over the young man. If he was unable to renounce the false sense of security, self-assurance, and self-sufficiency he derived from his fortune, Jesus knew the young man would be incapable of serving God as one of his disciples. For when Jesus said, "no one can serve two masters," he did not mean that it was unwise to serve two masters, but that, in the end, it was impossible.

LIVING SIMPLY

> This session is designed to explore the concept of voluntary simplicity.

GETTING STARTED

To have or not to have is a big question. Almost everything in our consumer-driven society tells us that we should want more and get more. But in a new trend, those of us who voluntarily do without are seen as the wave of the future.

DAVID

If Madison Avenue were to print a "Ten Most Wanted" poster, David Sweet's picture would be on it. David, a mild-mannered city inspector and father of two, isn't exactly doing his part to fuel the engines of commerce these days. "I don't buy much stuff anymore," he admits. "I made a declaration to myself that I have enough, that I really don't want any more than what I have in my life—so I don't aspire to better clothes or a nicer car."

Instead of the mall, David's idea of a good time is to meet with his cooperative work group. Each month, they gather at one of their member's houses to paint, do yard work, and make minor repairs. Afterwards, they relax with a potluck dinner. "There are

START Check in with each other and welcome newcomers. Ask how many are familiar with the concepts of living simply as an intentional lifestyle.

CASE STUDY

David
Read the case study of David or use an experience of your own to look at the issue of voluntary simplicity. What do you know about the voluntary simplicity movement? Have you tried any of its principles? What did you do? Have you been happy with the results?

DISCUSS

If you have read *Your Money or Your Life,* give a short synopsis of its content. Was there any advice contained within the book that you really took to heart? What does *simple* mean to you?

SMALL GROUP

Traveling Light

Sit in a circle and play this introduction game. The first person will introduce him or herself and name an item (beginning with the letter A) he or she would take on a camping trip or vacation. ("My name is Rita, and I'd take a bed with me.") The adjacent person adds his name and a new item to the list ("My name is Tom, and I'm bringing a bed and a canoe.") Continue around the circle until everyone is introduced.

BIBLE

Read Mark 6:6b-13. What items did the disciples bring on their mission? Would you feel comfortable setting out on a journey with what the disciples were allowed to take with them? What was Jesus trying to teach the disciples by allowing them only these meager provisions? What is the significance of the disciples carrying only one tunic? How were they to decide whether to stay in a particular home?

millions of people whose ideas reflect these values, but they don't understand they're part of a huge movement," says David. "They feel isolated, strange. They need to know there's lots of other people feeling the same way. Creating community," he adds, "is absolutely critical."

Guided by the book, *Your Money or Your Life* by Joe Dominguez and Vicki Robin (Viking Penguin, 1992), David is reducing his debt and plans to retire within ten years. "Before, I felt I was often spending my time and money and energy on things that weren't important to me," he said. "Now I know exactly what I'm spending and exactly how long I had to work to get it."

TRAVELING LIGHT

Jesus would have made a lousy scout master. In Mark 6:6b-13, he sent out his disciples on a mission woefully unprepared, from our perspective. He made no allowance for bread or a bag or even spending money. Instead, the disciples were to take nothing with them except a staff, a pair of sandals, and one tunic—not a freeze-dried packet of stroganoff or a Swiss army knife among them.

Instead of a backpack full of camping gear, they had to learn to rely upon God for their provision. Lacking even a second tunic to ward off the night's chill, they depended on the hospitality of strangers for food and lodging. Enter the first household in which you are welcomed, Jesus said. Not the one with the best food, or the softest bed, or the greatest prestige, but the first to receive your proclamation with gladness. And so they departed on what was reported as a successful trip. "They cast out many demons, and anointed with oil many who were sick and healed them" (6:13). Luke adds that they brought "the good news ... everywhere" (Luke 9:6).

THE MIRACULOUS FEEDING

One wonders how their journey changed the disciples. Had they learned to trust God's gracious providence? Having experienced life as a pure gift, as an abundance, were they able to discard the anxiety that haunts all of us? That would have made for a happy ending, but the Bible is a record of human experience, not of fairy tales.

It is not coincidental that the miraculous feeding of the five thousand (Luke 9:10-17) took place immediately upon the disciples' return. When Jesus told them to provide dinner for the crowd, they were filled with consternation. Their experience of God's provision apparently was already a distant memory. "We have no more than five loaves and two fish," they anxiously protested. In response, Jesus illustrated once more for them the abundance of God. All were fed, we are told, with twelve baskets of food left over. Perhaps, when the last basket had been gathered, Jesus turned to his sheepish disciples and smiled. *"Would they ever learn?"* he must have wondered.

SIMPLIFY! SIMPLIFY!

Ancient history? Again we fast forward a couple of millennia. Millions of Americans are following Jesus' prescription for anxiety by lightening their load. Together they are redefining the meaning of abundance by

DISCUSS

Recall the burgeoning list of stuff you accumulated for your trip in the introduction exercise. How much of it was essential? practical? easy to carry? possible to use? impossible to use? Think of an experience in which you did overpack and had to hassle with a lot of stuff you either didn't need or didn't use. Compare that to the disciples' experience of traveling very light. Have you ever had a similar experience where you had to make do with very little? Which was easier—having too little stuff or too much? What did you learn?

LOOK CLOSER

Miraculous Feeding
Read Luke 9:10-17.
Use a Bible commentary to explore the passage further. Compare and contrast this text with the miraculous gift of manna God provided for Israel in the wilderness (Exodus 16:1-21). How are the stories similar? Do you think the crowd surrounding Jesus and the disciples remembered the gift Israel had received in the wilderness when they themselves were witness to another miraculous feeding? What does each text have to teach us about the abundance of God?

Why do you suppose Luke chose to follow the story of the mission of the disciples with the feeding of the five thousand? What is the relationship between the two? Judging from the disciples' response to Jesus' request that they prepare dinner for the crowd, had they learned to trust in God's provision?

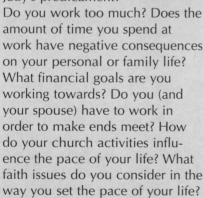
simplifying their lifestyles, trading in the material rewards of society's good life for individual and family pursuits. Dubbed "voluntary simplicity," the movement is prompting a growing number of people tired of the commute, the power lunches, and the "dressing for success," to turn their backs on the rat race.

BOB AND JUDY

To say Bob is an early riser is an understatement. Before sunrise, he is already at work operating a lathe, a job that demands 60 hours of his time each week. Meanwhile, his wife Judy, having fed their three small children and dropped them off at daycare, has arrived at her office by 7:30 A.M., where she works 50 hours a week as a stockbroker. Together, Bob and Judy earn over six figures a year. Yet their financial success exacts a price—neglected children, a strained marriage, and personal stress. They make a lot of money, but when do they enjoy it?

"DIS-EASE"

There is evidence that the increasing popularity of voluntary simplicity coincides with a growing dissatisfaction with materialism. According to a nationwide poll conducted by the Merck Famay Fund, 89 percent of women and 75 percent of men agreed with the statement that, as a society, we are addicted to shopping. Furthermore, 75 percent of the women and 69 percent of the men felt that "consuming is a substitute for what's missing in our lives." When asked what changes would be needed in order for their life to be more fulfilling, the majority cited more time spent with family and friends, less stress, and the opportunity to contribute to their community.

Not surprisingly, given their level of "dis-ease" with their current lifestyles, 28 percent had already made changes in their lives during the past five years that had resulted in a reduced salary. Their three most popular methods of "downshifting" were changing to less stressful, lower-paying employment; putting in fewer hours at work; and quitting their job outside of the home. The majority were happy with their simplified lifestyle.

JIM AND JANET

Janet Lui, a financial advisor, and her husband, Jim, an electrical engineer, had become dissatisfied with their fast-paced life in California. "There was so much pressure to accumulate things, and we found that wasn't making us happy," Janet said. So they decided to simplify. In 1990, the Lius spent $40,000 a year on their house, cars, and food. By 1996, after moving to Oregon, they'd been able to reduce the amount of income they needed to $30,000. At the same time, they steadily reduced their debt while increasing their savings. Eventually, they shifted to part-time work. Though they make do with less, they feel the additional family time they now enjoy with their eight-year-old daughter is worth the sacrifice.

THE FISHERMAN AND THE BUSINESSMAN

Perhaps, if Jesus were here today, he would tell us the parable of the businessman and the fisherman. It goes like this: "One day a businessman on vacation in a Mexican seaside resort was watching a fisherman unload a small catch of fish. 'Why don't you stay out at sea longer and bring in more fish?' he asked. 'Because I like to spend my time playing with my children, taking a siesta with my wife, and visiting with my friends,' replied the fisherman. The American scoffed. 'If you worked harder, you could buy a second fishing boat, then a whole fleet. Eventually you'd head up a large corporation, list it on Wall Street, and become a rich man.' 'And then, señor?' 'Then comes the best part,' the businessman replied. 'You retire, move to a Mexican fishing village, and spend the day playing with your grandchildren, taking a siesta with your wife, and visiting with your friends.'"

TWO WAYS TO BE RICH

This simple parable goes to the core of the principle underlying voluntary simplicity—that there are two paths to wealth: earn more or want less. The concept is hardly novel. In the early 1900's, naturalist Henry David Thoreau (1817-1862) wrote, "That man is the richest whose pleasures are the cheapest." Later the English author, G. K. Chesterton (1874-1936) would concur. "There are two ways to get enough," he said. "One is to continue to accumulate more. The other is to desire less." But perhaps the philosophy was best summed up by the anonymous sage who observed,

"There are two ways to be rich: acquire great wealth or acquire few needs."

At its heart, the principle is an affirmation that the best things in life truly are free. The secret to living is, rather than setting our hopes in material gratification, to develop an appreciation for the abundance of God. Jesus, of course, had said something similar many years ago. "Do not worry, saying, 'What will we eat?' or 'What will we drink?' or 'What will we wear?'" he counseled. "For it is the Gentiles who strive for all these things; and indeed your heavenly Father knows that you need all these things. But strive first for the kingdom of God and his righteousness, and all these things will be given to you as well" (Matthew 6:31-33).

CHRISTIAN COMMUNALISM

From the beginning, the early church sought to incorporate Jesus' understanding of prosperity into its daily existence. Whereas the Gentiles were preoccupied with prestige and power as measured by the world, an elder or a bishop was not to be "a lover of money" (1 Timothy 3:3; Titus 1:7). Instead, Christians were to use their God-given resources for the betterment of others. Consequently, they practiced a communal form of welfare, becoming renowned for their caring and compassion.

Acts 4:32-37 relates one model of mutual sharing, which points out the concern the early church had for persons whose lives were ones of involuntary simplicity—the have-nots of the community. As long as they took care of each other, "there was not a needy person among them" (4:34).

When they became deceitful and failed to truly take care of each other, the results

Read Matthew 6:31-33. Are you afflicted by anxiety? Do you worry about money? What is Jesus' message for you? What does it mean to "strive for the kingdom of God?" How is your church "striving for the kingdom of God?" How is your family "striving for the kingdom of God?" How are you personally "striving for the kingdom of God?"

Christian Communalism
Divide these Scriptures among you: 1 Timothy 3:3; Titus 1:7; Acts 6:1-7; Acts 4:32-37; Acts 5:1-11; Acts 6:1-7; Romans 12:13, 20; Romans 15:26; and 2 Corinthians 8:9. Together, formulate a composite picture of this type of early Christian community. What was the primitive church's attitude concerning money? In which types of charitable acts did the first Christians engage? How did they use their resources? What attitude was expected of these Christians regarding personal wealth? Was their giving required? In an ancient milieu not noted for its charity, what was the motivation behind Christian compassion? Can you relate to any of the persons or situations? If so, who? how? Is this model appropriate or possible for the church today? for an individual or family? for you? Explain.

LOOK CLOSER

Look again at Romans 12:20 and consider the Scripture's message about doing good to one's enemies. How does this fit into the practice of charity? of voluntary simplicity? Do you think you should do good to an enemy or a stranger? If you make a sacrifice for your own good or the good of your family, is that enough or are you also obligated by the Scriptures to extend yourself on behalf of others? Explain.

CLOSE

Find a partner and share with one another what one step you would feel comfortable taking in the coming weeks to begin changing current consumption or spending habits.

Close by praying for each other and for those for whom simplicity is not voluntary.

were disasterous. The unfortunate Ananias and Sapphira, who were not obligated to give up their belongings, separately lied about the extent of their gift, even though it was voluntary. When Peter caught them and confronted the lie, each one fell dead at his feet. That made an impression on everyone! (Acts 5:1-11).

In Acts 6:1-7, the first Christian officers were elected to ensure that the daily distribution of bread was fair and that all received their portion. This, too, reflected a concern for those whose lives did not include the luxury of deciding upon simplicity. In Romans 12:13 and 15:26, we find evidence that their generosity extended not just to the members of their own community, but to outsiders as well.

Biblical Studies 101: Heaping Hot Coals

Paul's remark in Romans 12:20 includes what sounds to our ears like a vindictive remark about being kind to an enemy. "By doing this [good deed] you will heap burning coals on their heads." Is Paul urging his readers to do good in order to shame the recipient? Possibly. This quote of Proverbs 25:21-22 encourages the Christian to model love in the face of hostility; that act may embarrass or nudge the recipient to reconsider his or her own attitude.

In fact, in Romans 12:20, the apostle Paul says, "If your enemies are hungry, feed them; if they are thirsty, give them something to drink." They found justification for their acts of generosity in Christ's own overwhelming act of sacrifice on behalf of all; for "though he were rich, yet for our sakes he became poor, so that by his poverty you might become rich" (2 Corinthians 8:9). It is not enough, the gospel tells us, to decide to live simply; one must also become actively involved in ensuring that others may simply live.

WHAT ABOUT MONEY?

> This session is designed to look into attitudes and habits concerning money and spending.

GETTING STARTED

Counting the first glass of lemonade sold, the first babysitting job, the first dollar earned for chores around the house, the first payment for a paper route or grass-cutting job, think about how long you have been a "formal" or "informal" member of the work force. The time mounts up, doesn't it?

SHIRLEY

Greet one another and introduce guests and newcomers.

As an administrator, 29-year-old Shirley had a comfortable income. Yet she was always broke. Worst of all, she had no idea where her money went. It was as if she had a hole in her pocket. At month's end, her desperation would increase with her bills. She finally had to admit she was living beyond her means. As a result of her penchant for using plastic on a whim, she had run up a credit card debt of $8,000. Then there was the car payment on that great-looking SUV that was equal to almost half her rent and the last of her school loans. She had no savings, no self-funded retirement, and no equity. As her financial world slowly caved in around her, she became para-

How much have you earned in your lifetime? Calculate roughly the amount of money that has come and gone through your hands since you folded your first newspaper or had your first babysitting job. You may find the total somewhat surprising. Then figure out how much you have to show for the money you've earned. First compile your assets and then subtract your liabilities. Are you satisfied with the results? Have you been following sound financial principles to this point or have you spent a lot of money with nothing to show for it?

lyzed with fear and indecision. *How,* she worried, *am I ever going to regain control over my finances and my life?*

FINANCIAL ILLITERACY

When it comes to personal finances, some, perhaps most, of us don't know any more than Shirley. According to the "Affluenza" website, 80 percent of Americans don't understand basic financial principles. As a result, many of us become overextended, sink into debt, and eventually declare bankruptcy.

The numbers aren't pretty. Americans shoulder $1 trillion in personal debt, spending 14 percent of our disposable income to repay it, the highest level since 1986. While credit card and household debt are at record highs, our savings continue to decline. In contrast to the Japanese who save 16 percent of their income, we save just four percent. The equation can end in bankruptcy; Americans filed over one million bankruptcies in 1996, three times as many as a decade ago.

FEAR

Suze Orman, author of *The 9 Steps to Financial Freedom* (Crown Publishers, Inc., 1997), speaks to thousands of people each year about personal finances. She has discovered that most of us know what we must do to free ourselves financially, but refuse to take action. While we're able to find time for everything else, we cringe at the thought of balancing our checkbook.

The truth is, she contends, we are afraid of money. It's like the proverbial 500-pound gorilla in the living room. Everyone is aware of its presence, but no one wants to deal with it. "Almost all of us have, at some level, fears or anxieties about money," she says, "but we rarely admit them to those around us. We may not admit them to ourselves." But until we are able to face those fears and, like Jacob wrestling with God, prevail, we will never be free of our financial anxiety.

DISCUSS

Fear
Why are we afraid to discuss money? What are your fears and anxieties about discussing money? About money itself? From where do those fears and anxieties originate? Is personal finance a taboo topic of conversation in your church? Why?

BUDGET

Financial experts advise us to start at the beginning. Our first step in putting a collar around that huge gorilla is to figure out our financial reality by keeping a detailed diary of our monthly expenses, recording *every* expenditure to the penny. At month's end, take a hard look at where your money has gone. Are you in the black or the red? Does your spending reflect your personal values? Are there places you could cut back? Are there other areas, such as charitable giving, where you should increase your effort? Based upon your findings, create a personal budget and stick to it. It will prove a key tool in helping you regain control of your finances.

MONEY = LIFE ENERGY

But what if you have a tendency to live beyond your means? Vicki Robin and Joe Dominquez, authors of *Your Money or Your Life* (Viking Penguin, 1992), offer a useful insight. They suggest we stop thinking about money as coin and paper, but as the time and effort it took to earn it. "Money," they say, "is something we chose to trade our life energy for." In other words, we literally "purchase" money with a portion of the limited number of hours we've been allotted.

SMALL GROUP

Budget
Bring to the session copies of classified ads for apartments, grocery items, clothing, cars. Include a mix of necessities (food) and optional purchases (electronic "toys"). Discuss your budgeting process. (If you do not make a budget, what's stopping you?) What is reasonable and what is not reasonable to pay for rent, transportation, clothing, entertainment, personal gadgets (refer to the ads). How do you prioritize your spending? For what items are you budgeting too much? For what things are you budgeting too little? What are some ways you save money? What are some of the ways you waste money? What is the single largest source of your debt? Are you living beyond your means? If so, do you think you need to do anything about it now? Explain.

DISCUSS

Money=Life Energy
How would you define "life energy"? Examine the equation "money = life energy." How does your perception change about consuming if you think of a purchase in terms of the number of hours of energy it took you to obtain it?

SMALL GROUP

Select something you own. For instance, your car or computer. Following the principle of "money = life energy," figure out the item's actual value. Begin by calculating your real hourly wage, then calculate the number of hours of life energy it required to purchase the item you've selected. How many hours or months did you have to work to pay for it? Was it worth it? If you were to apply the principle "money = life energy" to each purchase you consider, what impact would it have on your spending?

They encourage their readers to calculate their real hourly wage, including the hidden costs of commuting, clothing, lunches, and so on. Then, the next time you are tempted to purchase something, ask yourself, "Am I willing to trade the amount of my life energy required for this product?" You may decide you're willing to spend the life energy. On the other hand, you may decide the price is too high.

By staying within the parameters of our budget and faithfully practicing the principle "money = life energy," we're well on our way to financial solvency. It is then, when we start to have a little money, that an entirely new set of questions arise in regard to its proper use. How should I prioritize my spending? What are my responsibilities toward others? Can I still be a Christian and purchase that expensive set of wheels I saw the other day? The answers to these dilemmas won't be found in a financial investment portfolio, but in the Word of God.

THE RICH MAN

"As Jesus was setting out on a journey, a man ran up and knelt before him, and asked him, 'Good Teacher, what must I do to inherit eternal life?' And Jesus said to him, 'You know the commandments: You shall not murder; You shall not commit adultery; You shall not steal; You shall not bear false witness; You shall not defraud; Honor your father and mother.' The man said to him, 'Teacher, I have kept all these since my youth.' Jesus, looking at him, loved him and said, "Greed is good. Greed in all its forms; greed for life, money, love, knowledge, has marked the upward surge of mankind.' When he heard this, the young man smiled and went away filled with joy;

for he had many possessions.'"

Had you going there for a second, didn't I? The words substituted for Jesus' own are, of course, those spoken by wheeler-dealer Gordon Gecko in the movie *Wall Street*. In the film, Gecko is the personification of greed.

It is interesting to note the dissonance when his words are substituted for Jesus' own. The result is glaring because Jesus' admonishments concerning the lure of wealth are well-known. Although he did not condemn money outright, Jesus was wary of its ability to serve as a stumbling block for those seeking the Kingdom. By placing the choice between God or mammon before the rich man, he placed it before us as well. Who will you serve with your money: the idol of greed or the kingdom of God?

PROPHETIC TRADITION

In his concern for the proper place of money in our lives, Jesus stands squarely in his Hebrew tradition. As we've seen in previous sessions, Israel believed all blessings flowed from God's beneficence. Thus, the Israelites understood that the possession of money had to be tempered by a deep awareness of their dependence upon God and their responsibility to the less fortunate of our community.

Deuteronomy 24:10-22 contains a series of laws, each of which is designed to protect the poor. When Israel transgressed those laws by exploiting the needy, the prophets were quick to relay God's condemnation. In Amos 5, the prophet laments Israel's sin against the weak, accusing the powerful of "trampling on the poor" and "pushing aside the needy." Instead of empty worship

The Rich Man
Read Mark 10:17-27.
What did the rich man desire of Jesus? Imagine Jesus told you to sell all you have and give it to the poor. Would you do it? Could you do it? Does Jesus ever demand this of us today? Is it a sin to have a comfortable lifestyle when there are persons in the world (and in the next neighborhood) dying of starvation and want? Is it possible to be rich and still follow Jesus? Explain.

Prophetic Tradition
Read Deuteronomy 24:10-22 and Amos 5:10-13, 21-24. What evidence is there that Jesus' ministry was influenced by the prophetic tradition? If a prophet were to arrive in your town today, would he have grounds for accusing your community of mistreating the poor? for accusing you? Do we as a society "trample on the poor" and "push aside the needy?" What are you doing in your life to ensure that "justice rolls down like water, and righteousness like an ever-flowing stream?" If you are among the poor, is your only responsibility to receive or are you under the same mandate to give?

devoid of compassion, God requires justice to "roll down like waters, / and righteousness like an ever-flowing stream" (5:24).

LAZARUS AND "DIVES"

The prophetic concern for justice is evident in the teaching of Jesus, as well. In Luke 16:19-31, he relates the story of Lazarus. From the beginning of the parable, we know him to be the poor man lying outside the gate, which is often a place of commerce. But while the beggar is named, the rich man goes nameless. (Tradition has called him "Dives," meaning "rich man" in Latin.) Thus, Jesus has already foreshadowed the reversal of fortunes to come. For in the kingdom of God, it is the outcast who receives a name, while the one to whom society accords honor remains anonymous.

The reversal is illustrated in the story's two meal scenes. In the first, Lazarus is starving outside Dives's gate, even though Dives easily could have provided for him. In the second, both Lazarus and Dives have died and gone to their reward. The rich man looks up from his torment to see Lazarus "at the side" of Abraham (sometimes translated as "at the bosom"), a place of honor at a banquet.

The rich man does not accept his reversal of fortune easily. As he would with any errand boy, he asks Abraham to send Lazarus down with a drink of water. But the rules have changed. Having been rebuffed, the rich man then asks that Lazarus be sent to his brothers. Abraham replies, "If they do not listen to Moses and the prophets, neither will they be convinced even if someone rises from the dead." By placing the final taunt in the mouth of Abraham, Luke is witnessing to the continuity of Jesus' teaching regard-

SMALL GROUP

Lazarus and "Dives" Update and retell the story of Lazarus and "Dives" (Luke 16:19-31). Choose a modern counterpart to Lazarus, Dives, Dives's family members. You could act out the new story or retell it progressively (one person starts, another picks it up and adds more, and so on).

Why do you suppose Luke gives us the name of Lazarus, the poor man in the story, but not the name of the rich man? What is the rich man's attitude towards Lazarus? What is Abraham's attitude towards Lazarus? What crime has the rich man committed that he should suffer eternal punishment? Why does Abraham refuse to send Lazarus to the rich man's brothers? What was Jesus' point in telling this story? What new insights did you gain by examining the story in an updated version?

ing care of the marginalized with those of the Law and the Prophets.

THE PROPER USE OF MONEY

In contrast to the greed of Dives, Jesus often spoke of the correct use of money. In his encounter with Zaccheus, a tax collector who, if he followed in the presumed corruption of his trade, had cheated or extorted his clients, Jesus approves of Zaccheus' intention to give half his fortune to the poor and to reimburse fourfold anyone he had defrauded (Luke 19:1-10). After Zaccheus has made his pledge, Jesus proclaims, "Today salvation has come to this house." Dives and Zaccheus, both "sons of Abraham," were lost in their sin, but Zaccheus changed his heart and was found, and consequently, saved.

In the parable of the banquet (Luke 14:7-14), Jesus tells his listeners that, because God has done so, they too should provide a place at the table for "the poor, the crippled, the lame, and the blind." And finally, in Mark 12:41-44, Jesus commends the widow's offering given out of her poverty. Thus, it was not the amount of the offering that moved Jesus, for the others gave "large sums," but the humble spirit in which it was given. In short, Jesus taught that money is a tool to be used for the furtherance of the kingdom of God.

Proper Use
Read Luke 19:1-10. What was the nature of the transaction between Zaccheus and Jesus? Why, when Jesus didn't tell Zaccheus to sell all he had and give it to the poor, did he make the same demand of the rich man? What difference in attitude or circumstance was there, do you think, between the rich man and Zaccheus? Might that have made the difference in Jesus' advice? Explain.

Read Luke 4:1-13, 14:7-14, and 1 Timothy 6: 6-10. What do these texts have to teach us about the proper use of money? of gaining and keeping possessions? of healthy and unhealthy attitudes about possession? What is the difference between having money and loving money? How is the love of money the root of many forms of evil?

Re-examine your budget in light of these texts. Would Jesus approve of your fiscal priorities? How do you feel about your priorities? Is there anything you want to rethink or change?

Read Mark 12:41-44. Examine your own charitable giving. Are you giving out of your abundance or out of your poverty? How much are you willing to give back to God?

LOOK CLOSER Compare the attitude of the widow with that of the rich man unable to part with his wealth (Mark 10:17-27). Whom do you more closely resemble in your giving? Is it irresponsible to give sacrificially rather than save more for your future?

Read the texts in the Biblical Studies 101 box. How does a responsibility for a periodic tithe influence your current beliefs and patterns of giving?

Biblical Studies 101: Tithe

Read Deuteronomy 12:6-19; 14:22-29; 26:12-15; Amos 4:4. The widow's mite is a good context in which to consider the tithe. In the Hebrew Scriptures, Israelites were expected to give a tenth of their property or produce to those who had no land on which to grow crops—the Levite (priest), the sojourner, the fatherless, and the widowed. Specific practice of the tithe is difficult to identify with precision because the biblical record reports varying traditions. Nevertheless, both the tithe and the Year of Jubilee (Leviticus 25:8-17) were observed in recognition of God's ultimate ownership of the land and its fruits. While tithing is not a New Testament measure for giving, it can be a helpful starting point from which to begin your Christian stewardship.

SMALL GROUP

Gratitude

Either with a trusted partner or using a personal and private journal, talk through or write down your own attitude of gratitude. What do you believe God has given to you? For what do you owe God thanks? Is a "gospel of prosperity" (all my material goods are a blessing from God) a viable theology today, (since it would also suggest that those who do not have are lacking this blessing)? Explain.

CLOSE

Close by praying together: "Thank you, Lord Jesus, for all the gifts that you have given us. Create within us a heart of gratitude and a spirit of generosity. Awaken our awareness of your love for us and all of creation. And give us the courage to follow you no matter the cost. Amen."

GIVEN IN GRATITUDE

Jesus also taught that our decisions concerning money should flow from gratitude for what God has done. Until we fully understand the immensity of the debt we owe God for the food we eat, the water we drink, and the air we breathe, generosity will be still-born within us. Without an awareness of our dependence, we are no better than the unforgiving steward, who, though forgiven an unpayable debt, refused to forgive a trifling sum in comparison that was owed to him by another servant (Matthew 18:23-35).

It is a cautionary tale, a warning to remember the word Moses spoke to Israel: "Do not say to yourself, 'My power and the might of my own hand have gotten me this wealth.' But remember the LORD your God, for it is he who gives you power to get wealth. . . . If you do forget the LORD your God and follow other gods to serve and worship them, I solemnly warn you today that you shall surely perish" (Deuteronomy 8:17-19). Those "other gods" come in many guises, often related to money.

WASTE NOT, WANT NOT

This session will explore the means and costs of waste and the religious implications of being poor caretakers of what God provides.

SETTING STARTED

In previous chapters you have explored what you have, what you need, and what you obtain. Now think: How much of all that do you waste? Whatever the amount, you have a lot of company. We fritter away a lot!

JUST THE FACTS

- Ford's sports utility vehicle, the Excursion, weighs nearly a ton and gets 12 miles to a gallon of gas. (Ford has recently also announced plans to become more environmentally-friendly and safer with their large vehicles.)
- The average American consumes five times as much as an average Mexican, 10 times as much as an average Chinese, and 30 times as much as the average person in India.
- America's total annual waste would fill a convoy of garbage trucks able to reach around the globe six times.
- Every three months, Americans throw away enough aluminum to rebuild the entire commercial air fleet.
- Each year, Americans discard enough polystyrene cups to circle the globe 436 times.

START Take a few minutes to check in with each other and to welcome and introduce guests. Think about all you throw away, buy without using completely or at all, and waste (including water in the shower or for brushing your teeth, lights left on, newspapers and magazines unread, and so on). How much is there? More than you realized?

DISCUSS Choose a common product, such as an automobile, watch, tennis shoe, or telephone. Answer these following questions about that item: What resources were used to create the product? Are the resources renewable or nonrenewable?

Who makes the product and where? How likely is it that the workers who build the product, also own the product? Who buys the product? Is the product easy or difficult to repair? What happens to the product at the end of its life? What is the environmental impact of the product?

Now make a list of everyday items that are easy to repair and those that are difficult to repair. Who benefits from products that can be repaired, and why? Who benefits when a product is made so that it must be replaced after a short period of time? Would you be willing to spend more money on a product that is less environmentally harmful than the one you are currently using?

STEWARDS OF CREATION

As the saying goes, not all trivia is trivial. In this session, we will examine some of the attitudes we hold about abundance that hinder God's *shalom*, the wholeness and peace intended for Creation. Called to be faithful stewards of that Creation, too often our assumptions concerning money have resulted in destruction and waste. But before confronting our misguided beliefs, we turn to the biblical concept of stewardship.

A steward was in charge of the affairs of a large household. It was his duty to provide service at the master's table, oversee the other household staff, and manage the household expenses. In Hebrew, the word *steward* literally meant "man over the house." Consequently, the position of steward entailed a great deal of responsibility. In Genesis, the role of steward is used to describe our relationship with God's Creation. We were placed in the garden of Eden to "till and keep it" (2:15). For centuries, we interpreted this passage as carte blanche permission to subdue the earth and pillage its treasures.

Biblical Studies 101: The Dishonest Steward (Luke 16:1-9)

This parable is a very troublesome one to interpret, and Bible scholars do not all agree on its meaning. There are at least three ways to understand the steward and his actions. Of them, perhaps this carries the most weight: He was dishonest and in his manipulations with the clients, he continued to be dishonest. The point is not that the hearers of this parable should "go and do likewise" (meaning get what you can any way you can), but to be as clever and as prudent in securing their future in honest and righteous ways.

But isn't the principle figure of a parable usually a representation of God or of Jesus? This dishonest steward can't be the God-figure here—and he isn't. The steward takes on the character of another familiar figure in Jewish folklore: the trickster. Jesus' hearers would realize that the trickster would discern that in a crisis, he must be shrewd and decisive. The message for us: When we stake our claim with the claim of the Kingdom we must also respond with intelligence and urgency.

Like the dishonest manager, we squander what is not ours (Luke 16:1-9). Jesus closed the parable by saying, "Whoever is faithful in very little is faithful also in much; and whoever is dishonest in a very little is dishonest also in much." He cautions us to take care of the little that has been left in our care in this life, or else we may not be trusted with the riches of the life to come. For Jesus knew how easily stewardship can be derailed by our misconceptions about money.

MONEY AS POWER

The first misconception foisted upon us by our culture is that money equals power. An evening of television viewing or a cursory glance at the latest issue of *Vogue* is all the evidence needed to illustrate that the rich live in a rarefied realm of status and influence. Surrounded by luxury and privilege, it is easy to become convinced you need not be beholden to anyone, not even God.

Even our Bible heroes are not immune. In 1 Kings 9:1-9, God promised King Solomon a long and successful reign. But God's covenant with Solomon contained a caveat: he must serve no other gods. In return, "King Solomon excelled all the kings of the earth in riches and in wisdom" (1 Kings 10:23).

However, Solomon did not uphold his end of the pledge. Against the expressed desire of God, he became infatuated with foreign women, taking many as his wives. As God had feared, Solomon's wives seduced him into the worship of rival gods. At their bidding, Solomon constructed sanctuaries to their deities, high places where his wives burnt incense and worshiped. Solomon had forgotten

LOOK CLOSER

Read Luke 16:1-9. Have a Bible commentary on hand to help explain this passage. Why did Jesus tell his disciples the parable of the dishonest manager? Is the manager a favorable or an unfavorable character? Why does the master upon his return commend the dishonest manager? Who do you identify with in the story: the master, the debtors, or the manager? What meaning does Jesus draw out of the parable in verses 8-9? How does the parable relate to the theme of stewardship?

CASE STUDY

Use the dishonest steward, an experience of your own, or one of these examples to explore the idea of being faithful in much (Luke 16:10-13).

- The office manager jealously guards the supply closet against pilfering. The other employees resent the hassle; the boss goes to have a word with the manager. What might the boss have to say?
- You and your spouse need a larger house because a child is on the way, but your income will decrease when Mom works only part-time. How can you maximize your resources to get what you want?

BIBLE

Money as Power
Read 1 Kings 9:1-9 and 12:17-20. Describe the covenant between God and Solomon. How did Solomon break the covenant? What was the result? How, for Solomon, was money power, and how was that power abused or exploited? What does the tragedy of Israel tell us about our own stewardship?

God's words and mistaken the trappings of wealth for the power to do as he pleased. But God soon reminded him of the source of true power, punishing Solomon by dethroning his son, Rehoboam, in favor of Jeroboam (1 Kings 12:17-20). Solomon had broken his covenant with God and, as a result, the wealth that had been placed in his care and of his descendants was lost.

We might learn a lesson from the division of Israel. God has placed us in a position of responsibility as stewards of the environment, gifting us in turn with the unparalleled abundance of creation. But like Solomon, we too have become enamored of our own power, exploiting the world's resources without thought to the consequences. The pollution of our skies, seas, and land have been the inevitable result.

Put simply, the earth can no longer withstand our society's materialistic conception of the abundant life. With less than five percent of the world's population, the United States consumes 25 percent of the globe's resources. In 1997, Northwest Environmental Watch estimated that if the rest of the world were to exhaust natural resources at the same rate as Americans—approximately 120 pounds a day per capita—three more earths would be needed to handle the demand. It proves the point Mahatma Gandhi once made when he said, "The world has enough for everyone's need, but not for everyone's greed." Without a return to the responsible stewardship to which God entrusted us, we, like Adam and Eve before us, will be driven from Paradise. The difference is that we have no where else to go.

MONEY AS SELF-FULFILLMENT

The second cultural misconception we fall victim to concerning money is that we are free to use our wealth for our own fulfillment, rather than for the benefit of our community. It is this narcissistic tendency within each of us Jesus addressed in the parable of the prodigal or wasteful son (Luke 15:11-32).

It begins with an ancient and extreme *faux pas*. According to Jewish custom, the dispensation of the father's wealth should not have occurred prior to his death. But his younger son couldn't wait for nature to take its course. Instead, he demanded his inheritance, which in essence said to the father and the whole community, "I regard you as dead." But his father gave his son what he asked. Having received it, he journeyed to a "distant land," the land of the Gentiles. There he squandered his property in dissolute living. Eventually, he was reduced to tending pigs, an animal his religion regarded as unclean and an occupation that was the lowest of the low. Finally coming to his senses, the son dragged himself home, arriving destitute, hungry, and ashamed.

AN UNPAYABLE DEBT

One wonders how the parable might have ended had the younger brother had access to a MasterCard. Judging by the amount of credit card debt accumulated by Americans, it would have probably only delayed the inevitable. For with the prevalence of easy credit and our "pay later" attitude, we too are squandering our inheritance. According to federal statistics, during 1998, credit card debt doubled to $22.5 billion. Financial experts predict the trend

Self-fulfillment
Read Luke 15:11-32 and a commentary on the passage in a Bible commentary. This story is very rich in imagery and implication for its presentation of the father as generous, forgiving, and ultimately hospitable. What is the meaning of the word *prodigal*? Did the younger son have the right to demand his inheritance? What were the implications of his leaving home and frittering away his portion of the family estate? of returning and having the possibility of benefiting from the remaining estate? How did the older brother figure in the story? How did he behave and how did he feel? Do you relate to anyone? Why?

CASE STUDY
Use the story's characters to explore similar events in your own life. Have you ever squandered your property in "dissolute living"? What was the result? In your own family dynamics, are you the "elder son" or the "younger brother?" Do you have any lifestyle habits that waste your financial resources? Could you live a contented life with fewer material possessions? What personal and social changes would you be willing to consider?

An Unpayable Debt
How many credit cards do you have? Have credit cards made it possible for you to spend beyond your means? Has your personal credit card debt grown during the past five years? Is this debt a problem?

The average balance-carrying household owes $7,564 on its credit cards. How does your credit card debt compare? If you pay interest later to have your purchase now, do you consider that wasteful? Explain. Imagine if you didn't have credit cards. How would that alter your spending habits? How can you resist all the appeals for easy credit you receive?

to accelerate further with the widespread acceptance of shopping on the internet.

The waste resulting from our penchant for plastic is horrendous. Fewer than one-third of Americans pay off their credit card balance at the end of the month. The rest continue to carry it over, paying interest rates as high as 19 percent. Consequently, a large portion of their income is wasted. For example, if you were to make just minimum payments on an average credit card debt of $2,000, it would take 11 years to repay and cost an additional $1,900 in interest.

Biblical Studies 101: Forgive Us Our Debts

The Old Testament stands firmly against economic injustice, including usury. In Exodus 22:25-27, the Lord instructs Moses to tell the Israelites that they are forbidden to charge interest on loans to the poor. The injunction reads: "If you lend money to my people, to the poor among you, you shall not deal with them as a creditor; you shall not exact interest from them." In the same passage, in the case of a loan made to a poor neighbor, the Israelites are admonished to return a garment handed over as pledge before sunset, "so that your neighbor may sleep in the cloak and bless you." The New Testament is also wary of the practice of charging interest on loans. In Luke 6:34-36, Jesus tells his disciples to "love your enemies, do good, and lend, expecting nothing in return."

FORGIVE US OUR DEBTS

Forgive Us Our Debts
How much do you actually know about your credit cards? Take one from your purse or wallet. Answer the following questions: Who is the lender? How much is your annual fee? What is the interest rate on your credit card? Is there a fee for cash advances? What is the interest rate on a transferred balance? How much would a late payment cost you? What is the limit of credit available on your card?

As in any revolution, there are winners and there are losers. What do you do if you end up on the losing side of the credit card revolution? The first step must be an honest appraisal of your financial position. How much in debt are you? Once you have an answer, you are ready to embark on a debt management program.

Financial guru Suze Orman offers a helpful ten-point credit card debt reduction strategy:

- If you are in credit card trouble, cut up the cards immediately.
- Reduce the cost of interest by paying more than the minimum payment.

- Pay off the debt that carries the highest interest rate first and then the rest in descending order.
- Negotiate the best interest rates available, even if it means changing credit cards every six months.
- Understand your credit card fees.
- Honor all debts equally.
- When your debt carrying the highest interest rate has been paid, add that payment to the amount you are paying on the debt with the second highest interest rate.
- Contact the National Foundation for Consumer Credit (800-388-2227; *www.nfcc.org*) for further assistance.
- Never allow yourself to get in credit card debt again.
- Once out of debt, use your money to build your future.

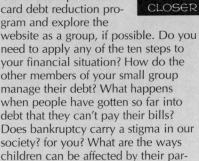

LOOK CLOSER

Review together Suze Orman's ten-point credit card debt reduction program and explore the website as a group, if possible. Do you need to apply any of the ten steps to your financial situation? How do the other members of your small group manage their debt? What happens when people have gotten so far into debt that they can't pay their bills? Does bankruptcy carry a stigma in our society? for you? What are the ways children can be affected by their parents' debt?

MONEY AS SECURITY

Our third misconception is that money can purchase security. Thus, we hoard our resources, failing to put them to work for others. Like the older son in the story of the prodigal, we clench our inheritance tightly, afraid to share lest we be left penniless.

CASE STUDY

Money as Security
Use the anecdote or an experience of your own to examine the waste of hoarding. Have you ever thought about hoarding as waste? What else does it waste besides the use of the resource itself? (For example, how might the miser have put his time to other use if he didn't dig up and count his money each night? He will probably spend his emotions now in fretting and complaining; how might he better use his emotional energy?)

There is a story of such a man, a miser who sought security in material possessions. Each night, he'd sneak into his backyard to unearth a strongbox he'd buried. After counting his money, he'd rebury the box until the next day. He continued this routine for years, until one night he discovered a hole where his treasure had been. Realizing his money had been stolen, he began to wail. His cries awoke his neighbor, who came running. But upon learning the miser's plight, the neighbor turned away. "What's all the fuss about," he said to himself. "He wasn't using the money for anything anyway." This simple little story is illustrative of the biblical attitude towards abundance. Money is

BIBLE

Read Luke 12:13-21. Why would Luke chose to introduce the parable of the rich fool with a query concerning inheritance? What's the connection? Why is the rich man portrayed as foolish? Wasn't he just being a good steward by building larger barns? Does Jesus mean that we shouldn't save for the future? According to Jesus, is it possible to store up treasure and still be on good terms with God? If we spend our time storing up treasure for ourselves, could that be time wasted? If so, how? When you die, to whom will all your stuff belong ?

CLOSE

If possible, go outside. Spend a minute in silence, becoming aware of the beauty of creation around you. Then pray the following prayer: "God of Creation, thank you for the gift of our earth. Forgive us our failures as stewards of your Creation. Show us the ways we waste and exploit, and create in us the will to change that behavior. With your Holy Spirit, empower us to keep faithfully our covenant. Guide us, O Lord. Show us the ways in which we can care daily for our environment, so that we may leave a legacy of responsible stewardship to our children; in Christ we pray. Amen."

not to be hoarded, but is a tool to be used compassionately on behalf of others. One might argue that failing to use it wisely is to waste it.

Of course, Jesus tells a similar tale. The parable of the rich fool (Luke 12:13-21) is introduced by an exchange between Jesus and a member of the crowd, apparently another one of those pesky younger brothers. "Teacher!" he shouted. "Tell my brother to divide the family inheritance with me." Jesus responded by cautioning him against seeking security in money. "Take care!" he said. "Be on your guard against all kinds of greed; for one's life does not consist in the abundance of possessions." He then related the story of the rich fool.

The rich man's harvest had been so large that he had had to tear down his barns to build larger ones. The thought of sharing his good fortune with others never crossed his mind. Instead, he eagerly anticipated his own pleasure. *Now,* he thought, *I can "relax, eat, drink, and be merry."* But God had other plans, demanding the man's life that very night. "And the things you have prepared, whose will they be?" asked God.

The reversal could not have been more pronounced. The rich fool, like the prodigal, forfeited his inheritance. "So it is," warns Jesus, "with those who store up treasures for themselves but are not rich towards God." Waste not, want not.

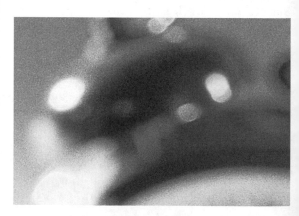

ETHICS OF ABUNDANCE

> This session is designed to examine the ethics of having enough to live and something to give, and to review how choices are made about having and using our personal resources.

GETTING STARTED

It is entirely possible to have too little; is it possible to have too much? How do we evaluate how much is too much and how little is too little? What priorities, attitudes, and beliefs factor in to the way we decide?

"I'M THINKING!"

Jack Benny was so tight with a dollar, he squeaked when he walked. It was his schtick, his persona as a comedian, and his audience loved it. A notorious skinflint, each week he would regale a new audience with penny-pinching jokes. In one of his most famous skits, he was accosted by a man with a gun. "Your money or your life?" the robber shouted. The viewers would begin to chuckle. In his patented move, Benny would slowly turn to the onlookers, one hand on his chin in thought, a look of concentration on his face. "Well?" demanded the robber. In exasperation, Benny responded, "I'm thinking. I'm thinking."

START — Offer a prayer, expressing your concerns to God about the role money plays in your life.

"I'm Thinking"
Complete the sentence: "Money is. . . ." Explore some of the insights you have received in the course of this study by answering the following questions: Are most of your answers concerning money positive or negative? What is your definition of *enough*? When does enough become too much? What are you expected to give back to God? to your community? your family? to others? What is the abundant life for you? Has your definition of the abundant life changed from when you started this study?

The Crux
In groups of two or three develop an affirmation of faith in regard to the abundant life to which you can all agree. For examples of affirmations of faith, see your denomination's hymnal or worship book. Share your affirmation of faith with the other groups. Are their any similarities? any surprises? any new insights?

Counterculture

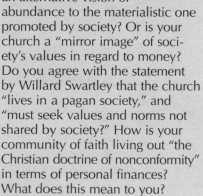

Does your church offer an alternative vision of abundance to the materialistic one promoted by society? Or is your church a "mirror image" of society's values in regard to money? Do you agree with the statement by Willard Swartley that the church "lives in a pagan society," and "must seek values and norms not shared by society?" How is your community of faith living out "the Christian doctrine of nonconformity" in terms of personal finances? What does this mean to you?

Are we in danger of domesticating the Bible's message concerning money? In one or two sentences, write a statement that expresses the biblical perspective on money. Take into account some of the following Scriptures that stress the radical nature of the biblical witness: Luke 1:46-56; 6:20-26; Mark 8:34-37; 10:28-31

THE CRUX OF THE MATTER

"Your money or your life?" In many ways, it's the decision facing us all, the dilemma of our times. It is the question we've been wrestling with together these past few weeks: "What is the abundant life?" Is it a life in which our relationship with God takes center stage or a life of seeking after material satisfaction? It is the question Jesus posed when he asked his followers whom they served—God or mammon.

Of course, as Christians, there can be no debate. We are called to love and serve God with all our heart, with all our soul, and with all our might. All else is of secondary importance. It is a decision that will, at times, place us in conflict with the culture in which we live. For in a society that worships wealth and measures self-worth in possessions, the assertion that we have no right to our money, that whatever we have is a gift from God, that our possessions are simply tools to be used compassionately on behalf of others, is still revolutionary.

COUNTERCULTURE

Where will we find the strength to resist mammon's legions if not from the community of faith? But too often we have failed as a church to offer an alternative vision of abundance. Instead, we reflect a mirror image of society's values, grasping for position and power with the best of them. As a result, the church has become a sadly irrelevant ethical guide. For as Willard Swartley, a New Testament scholar, once wrote, "If it has not already done so, the church must recognize that it lives in a pagan society; it must seek for values and norms not shared by society. In short, it will either recover the Christian doctrine of nonconformity or cease to have any authentic Christian voice."

CULTURAL NONCONFORMITY

The church has a rich tradition of going its own way when it comes to monetary matters. As mentioned previously, the early Christian community practiced a type of communal welfare, sharing what they had with others. In Acts 2:43-45, the believers are said to have "had all things in common." Apparently conversion entailed a divestiture of private property for those who wished to do so. For the text says, "They would sell their possessions and goods and distribute the proceeds to all, as any had need." Again in Acts 4 we read, "Everything they owned was held in common" (verse 32). Converts sold their land or houses and laid the proceeds at the feet of the apostles for distribution. Because of this generous practice, it is said "there was not a needy person among them" (verse 34).

There is evidence in the epistles that the charitable giving that characterized the early Christian churches also extended beyond the bounds of their community. In 2 Corinthians 8, the apostle Paul commended the churches of Macedonia for their generosity, testifying that they "voluntarily gave according to their means, and even beyond their means, begging us earnestly for the privilege of sharing in this ministry to the saints" (verses 3-4). He urged them to strike a fair balance between their abundance and the need of others (verses 13-14).

Nonconformity
Read the following passages describing the monetary practices of the early church: Acts 2:43-45; 4:32-34. What picture of the early church arises from these passages? Financially how does it compare to your own situation? Based on these Scriptures, should Christians divest themselves of their property by selling their property and giving it to the church? Should we adopt a communal model of stewardship? (Remember that this was still voluntary, not an all-or-nothing approach.) How does the early church's treatment of money challenge us today?

Read 2 Corinthians 8:1–9:15 and use a Bible commentary to explore the passage in more depth. What does it mean to excel in generous giving? Are you giving sacrificially? Are you following the biblical mandate of giving a tithe of your earnings? If not, what would be the consequences if you did? If you are tithing, how has the practice benefited you? After examining the amount you are giving to the church and others in need, have you concluded you are giving enough or is God asking more of you?

SMALL GROUP

Look especially at 2 Corinthians 8:12-14. In groups of two or three, play a giving game. The first person will address the one on his or her left with a question about giving: Would you be able to give __? (start small, either in terms of time, money, or other tangible resources). Person Two will decide if that gift is possible, then continue by asking the next person to the left a similar question, but increase the request slowly. Keep going until each person has hit his or her limit of ability or willingness to give. Where did each of you find the point at which the balance tipped from giving that was "doable" to burdensome?

DISCUSS

Finding Abundance
How can today's church recapture the early Christians' generous attitude toward money? Review the meaning of abundance as more than just the possession of money and stuff. How can you as an individual and a group help your church family find abundance?

In 2 Corinthians 9, Paul delivers what must be one of the first stewardship sermons, exhorting the Corinthian Christians to give generously to the community in Jerusalem. Evidently, this congregation was not well-acquainted with the notion of helping others, so Paul schooled the young church in the basic principles of Christian charity, saying, "The point is this: the one who sows sparingly will also reap sparingly, and the one who sows bountifully will also reap bountifully. Each of you must give as you have made up your mind, not reluctantly or under compulsion, for God loves a cheerful giver. And God is able to provide you with every blessing in abundance, so that by always having enough of everything, you may share abundantly in every good work" (9:6-8).

FINDING ABUNDANCE

How can today's church recapture the early Christians' generous, almost light-hearted attitude towards money? To begin with, we could implement what are called in the parlance of the voluntary simplicity movement, simplicity circles. These are nothing more than small groups of persons who commit to sharing their financial lives with one another. Members provide each other with encouragement to simplify, collective willpower in the face of consumer pressure, financial counsel, and a degree of economic accountability. Together they explore countercultural options, such as voluntary simplicity, shared property, cooperative housing, alternative patterns of work, and the decommercialization of relig-ious holidays. Finally, simplicity circles would serve as a vanguard for their community, faithfully seeking to live out the Christian understanding of abundance.

Do you think the topic of personal finances, such as how we earn and spend our money, should be discussed among brothers and sisters in Christ? How could the church help its members "decommercialize" their lives?

GLENN

This business about simplicity circles and voluntary giving is all well and good for you, but I don't have any discretionary money. I try to keep my expenses down, but I have to pay the rent and eat, and I need to have a little fun sometime. I'm certainly glad to hear that God doesn't want me to be burdened by giving, because I don't have anything to give. I really need what I have, and that's not selfish; it's just a fact of life for me.

Glenn
Use Glenn's example or something from your own experience to examine abundance when there seems to be none. If abundance is more than just the accumulation of possessions, how can Glenn understand what he does have to give? Glenn sounds a bit defensive about having to make a decision not to give. What is the church's obligation to honor a person's decisions about what and how much to give? our obligation to be honest and not hide behind "the church is always asking for money" as an excuse to not give?

CLOSING CHALLENGE

As provocative as the practice of communal sharing and voluntary simplicity might appear, they do not reflect the deeply radical nature of the biblical witness in regard to money. After all, the early church did not gather to debate the pros and cons of shared chariot ownership. Instead, together they implemented a subversive vision of economic equality. Extremes of wealth within

Challenge
Read James 2:1-13. Describe the problem from James's point of view. Is discrimination based upon appearance evident among your church fellowship?

the body of Christ was looked upon with distrust. In James 2:1-13, the damage wrought by such inequality is evident.

The church is taken to task for acts of favoritism toward its rich converts. The community of Jesus Christ was to be a place in which such worldly distinctions were banished. "Listen, my beloved brothers and sisters," James pleaded. "Has not God chosen the poor in the world to be rich in faith and to be heirs of the kingdom that he promised to those who love him? But you have dishonored the poor. . . . You do well if you really fulfill the royal law according to the scripture, 'You shall love your neighbor as yourself'" (2:5-6, 8).

As the preceding passage makes clear, by any standard of measurement, we have just begun to probe the countercultural implications of biblical abundance. In our effort to please others, we must guard against domesticating the biblical message and dispelling its challenge. In this study, the point has been made that the Bible, though wary of money's ability to undermine discipleship, nevertheless understands it to be amoral, simply a tool that can be used for either great good or great evil, depending on the hand that wields it.

We have pointed out that Jesus himself relied on monetary support for his mission.

Nor did he demand of everyone he met that they give all their money to the poor. But, that having been said, he did call some, such as his closest disciples and the rich young man, to a life of voluntary poverty. Thus the possibility that God may also be calling us to a life of voluntary poverty, or at least simplicity, must be taken seriously by anyone who would follow Jesus.

In the end, we have arrived back to our original question: What is the abundant life? How much is enough? What does God require of you financially? It is our fate as Christians never to be at ease with money. Instead, we are slated to wrestle daily with the role mammon plays in our lives, continuing all the while to bear witness to a vision of abundance at odds with the world.

EPIPHANY

Why it happened on that particular day, she couldn't say. All Roberta knew for sure was that at some point during the morning, she snapped. Perhaps it was the 30 e-mails demanding her attention the minute she walked in the door of her office that morning. Or it could have been the irritating summons of the phone, or the incessant vibration of her pager. Or maybe she was just fed up with lugging around her five-pound organizer, filled with to-do lists, phone logs, meeting maximizers, and five-year plans. Whatever the catalyst, Roberta suddenly knew she was tired of trying to keep up with the pace of her own life.

The following weekend, Roberta went on a personal retreat to sort out her feelings. During the next couple of days, she pondered the decisions she and her husband, Malcolm, had made during their marriage.

SMALL GROUP

Bring a copy of your church budget to class. Scrutinize the manner in which your church spends its money. Are your budget's priorities in keeping with the biblical understanding of abundance? Does your church set a stewardship example by giving to persons in need? Imagine if Jesus read your budget. What would his response be?

Every year churches purchase or design a stewardship campaign. As a group, develop a radical campaign based on the biblical definition of *abundance*. Would your end goal be to persuade people to tithe? How would you motivate people to give? What's your campaign slogan? symbol? How would you prioritize your church's spending?

CASE STUDY

Epiphany
Discuss Roberta's situation or one of your own experiences in examining your daily activities. Is your life a grind as Roberta's seemed to be? Is it work for you just to try to have fun? Are you in control of your stuff and your schedule or are they in control of you? How much of whatever hassle you face day to day is of your own creation (from not knowing how to say no or from poor planning, for example) and how much of it is beyond your control? Are you close to a "meltdown" as Roberta was? How can you recognize the signs and do something positive about it?

CASE STUDY

New Dream
Examine Roberta and Malcolm's solution to her epiphany or use an experience of your own. Their solution was very wide-ranging. Is something that extensive what you need? Having completed this study, are there any changes in store for your lifestyle? Do you need to simplify? If so, what steps could you take? Has your perception of the abundant life changed? Will you be handling your money any differently? Your other resources, such as time, emotional energy, devotional strength? Have your priorities changed? How will you be giving back to others and God?

CLOSE
Sing "Take My Life, and Let It Be Consecrated," then join together in prayer for discernment for how God wants you to live your life, do your work, and offer your gifts.

She realized they had bought into society's "more toys" approach to personal fulfillment. They had the requisite big house, the new cars, and the other accouterments of the American Dream. But something was missing. Both she and Malcolm worked high profile, stressful jobs that demanded most of their time and energy. As a result, they had all the rewards of success—except time with one another. By the end of her weekend, Roberta had reached a decision: it was time to step off the fast track.

THE NEW AMERICAN DREAM

When Roberta got home she told her husband of her desire for a less complicated life. To her surprise, he agreed. Together they determined they would simplify. The first thing they did was to take a long, hard look at their possessions, jettisoning anything they weren't using. With less stuff to store, they decided they would downsize by selling their house. They then moved from the suburbs to a coastal community in California. After finding employment, they rented a small condominium within walking distance of both their work and the ocean. Now, no longer commuting, they sold their cars, electing instead to rent a vehicle for weekend jaunts. Free of the expense of their home, their cars, and their commute, Roberta and her husband found they were able to live quite comfortably on their reduced income. No longer forced to leave the house at dawn to get to work, they linger over breakfast. In the evening, each is home in time for a walk on the beach. Roberta and Malcolm are once again living the American Dream, only this time, they're living it on their terms.

CASE STUDIES

Getting Started

Use any of these cases in place of or in addition to the cases in the sessions as a means of stimulating discussion.

Holiday Hype

What had been planned as a fun holiday outing was turning into a nightmare. *The traffic getting downtown is enough to make a grown woman cry*, Carol thought. Finding parking had been a quest suitable for Odysseus. Now she and her three children were pushing through the crowds, which stood spellbound in front of vast holiday displays. While the baby wailed, the twins, each pulling at one side of her coat, were trying to rip her down the middle like yesterday's wishbone. *I must have been nuts*, she thought, *to come shopping on the day after Thanksgiving.*

As they struggled toward the mall, Carol heard the sound of carols. The music came from a small group of people standing outside the mall entrance. *Finally*, she thought, *some Christmas cheer*. But when she and her children approached, Carol realized there was something decidedly odd about these carolers. They were women, each dressed like her grandmother on her worst day. One held a sign that read, "Cut Up Your Credit Card." And the lyrics they sang were a bit off as well. The tune was "Rudolph the Red-Nosed Reindeer," but the words they sang were, "Uh-oh, we're in the red, dear. . . "

One of the women handed Carol a "Buy Nothing Day" checklist. She urged Carol to use the checklist while shopping. It read: "Do I need it? How much do I already have? How much will I use it? Can I do without it? How will I dispose of it when I'm done using it? Are the resources that went into it renewable or nonrenewable?" Carol looked up from the card to find the woman still standing in front of her. "We're the Raging Grannies," she said warmly. "Welcome to the revolution."

- How would you respond to the message of the Raging Grannies?
- Do you think Christmas is too commercialized?
- What steps might we take to de-emphasize materialism during the Yuletide season?
- How much money do you spend on Christmas?

- Do you go into debt to buy presents for your loved ones?
- Does the celebration of your family's favorite Christmas rituals involve money?
- How does your church help you to keep Christmas in its proper perspective?

Voluntary Poverty

Jeremy stood in front of a cheering auditorium. Moments ago he had given his farewell address as president of the conference youth. It had been a sermon really, a stirring call to follow Jesus. The audience couldn't help but be moved. Most of the youth leaders in attendance had watched Jeremy, the son of a prominent clergyman, grow into a young man. He was strikingly handsome in a shy, endearing sort of way; the kind of person who turned heads when he entered a room. But even more impressive than his good looks was the commitment to Christ that glowed within him. Everyone who knew him thought it a foregone conclusion that he would follow his father into the ministry, maybe even become a bishop.

But Jeremy surprised the prognosticators. Instead of heading to seminary, he traveled east to India, where he spent time with a Christian missionary and his family. He lived among the people, sharing a small room with rats the size of house cats. Upon his return to the United States, Jeremy enrolled in pottery classes in the local community college. After two years of learning to throw pots, he returned to India. There he worked with an untouchable caste, the potters, helping them to form a collective through which to sell their earthenware pottery to Americans. Eventually, he married an Indian woman from a Christian family and together they had two children.

It's been ten years now since he moved to India. His ministry with the potters is thriving. Periodically he sends a cargo container filled with pots to his parents, who act as his unofficial distributor to local churches up and down the West Coast. In the letters he sends home to his supporters, he is effusive and filled with hope. Among the potters of India, Jeremy has found the abundant life.

- Have you ever felt God calling you to voluntary poverty?
- Why do some, such as Mother Teresa, seem to be called to a simple life of service while others are not?
- Are all Christians called to a simple life, but only a few have the courage to heed the call?
- What's the scariest thing God has ever asked you to do?

Abundance: Living Responsibly With God's Gifts

- Are we, by living a moderately comfortable American lifestyle, condemning others in the Third World to a life of poverty? Explain.
- How are you using your resources to address the injustice and hunger so prevalent in today's world?
- Jeremy sacrificed the pleasures of affluence to serve the poor. Would you? Explain.

A Mountain of Debt

Eric, 22, preferred a bohemian lifestyle. Much to his parents displeasure, he sported dreadlocks, bought his wardrobe at the local thrift shop, and had more body piercing than a pin cushion. Since he lived in an apartment the size of a shoe box, he spent most of his waking hours in a nearby coffee shop, sipping espresso and having long existential conversations with his friends. To cover his modest expenses, he waited tables at a vegetarian restaurant. His only vice was an insatiable appetite for CDs, a hunger that kept his credit card maxed. He didn't worry about it. After all, debt was the American way.

Eric met Kayla one night at a rave and, although their lifestyles could hardly have been less compatible, they instantly fell in love. Kayla loved money. A certified shopaholic, she spent a small fortune on her wardrobe. She knew she was living way beyond a receptionist's salary, but figured she'd pay it all back "someday."

It wasn't until they were engaged that Eric discovered that Kayla's passion for the high life had put her in debt $ 6,300. Suddenly Eric and Kayla were staring at a $10,000 debt. Neither was a whiz at money management, but both realized they could never start a family and continue to pay interest on their debt. *How*, they wondered, *were they ever going to escape from their debt trap?*

- What financial advice would you give Eric and Kayla concerning their debt?
- What is the amount of debt you are presently carrying? What is your net worth?
- How have you gotten into debt? What steps can you take to begin to eradicate that debt?
- What are the factors in American society pressuring us to assume debt?
- What is the biblical teaching concerning debt?
- Once you are out of debt, what are some of the precautions you can take to ensure that you will not slip back into debt?

Career Move

As the receptionist ushered her into the plush office, Carolyn fought to keep her nerves from betraying her. Jim, the man she'd come to see, greeted her warmly. As she sat down, she glanced at his brass nameplate. It read: "Vice President of Sales." She was here to interview for a position as sales representative with a financial services firm. It was showtime.

As Jim was introducing himself, Carolyn studied him intently. He was a big man, nearly six foot three. His clothes, though casual, were expensive. He wore a diamond ring, a gold watch and his hair had been permed into tight blond ringlets. Overall, his appearance bespoke success and money. She noticed one more thing: a cross hung around his neck.

He was telling her his own background. He'd begun his career as a high school coach and had gotten into sales by accident. When a friend suggested he try selling insurance, he gave it a shot. He proved a natural salesman. It wasn't too long before he was promoted, eventually landing his present position.

He asked Carolyn what her goals were, saying that if she didn't want to make at least $50,000 a year, not to bother with sales. It was too stressful. But if she applied herself and worked hard, there was no reason she couldn't earn six figures. Carolyn replied that it was important for her to have a sense of mission, that she'd like to be able to help people with their financial planning.

Jim agreed with her on the importance of having a higher purpose, sharing that God had blessed his own business success. Now he was enjoying all the pleasures life afforded, as well as supporting a Christian missionary in China. But, he said, if God ever wanted him to go back to coaching high school kids again for $26,000 a year, he wouldn't look back.

At the close of the interview, Carolyn thanked him for his time. On her way home, she wondered if Jim would have hired Jesus. *Probably not*, she thought. *He'd never have bothered to apply.*

- How important is it to you that your work have a sense of mission?
- Do you have a sense of vocation?
- In the context of your present employment, how are you in ministry?
- Would Jesus have wanted Carolyn to accept a position as financial sales representative?
- Is it possible to be both wealthy and Christian?
- Jim took great pride in sponsoring a missionary to China. As Christians, if we give a portion of our income to others, are we then free to spend the rest of our paycheck on our own desires?
- Is your sense of self-worth dependent upon the size of your salary?
- What income level is enough for you?

SERVICE LEARNING OPTIONS

Enhance your church's understanding of biblical abundance by implementing some of the service projects mentioned below:

IDEA #1: Simplicity Circle

Consider creating an on-going simplicity circle as a part of your church's Christian education program. The concept of simplicity circles was first introduced by Cecile Andrews in her book, *The Circle of Simplicity* (HarperCollins, 1997). To anyone with a background in small group ministry, the concept is familiar.

A simplicity circle is a group of individuals who covenant to meet together on a regular basis to discuss their concerns about money. Together, they encourage and inspire each other to simplify their lifestyles. Fellowship, study, prayer, and advocacy could all be part of the focus of your simplicity circle. In addition, the group would prove a valuable source of information on the topic of personal finances for your faith community.

IDEA #2: Financial Counseling

Everyone on occasion needs advice on their personal finances. For those who are deeply in debt, a place where they could talk with someone knowledgeable about money and the role it plays in their lives, could literally be a lifesaver. Consider meeting this need within your church family by creating a Christian financial counseling service. Stephen's Ministry, a lay program designed for voluntary care of church members, could serve as a model.

As in Stephen's Ministry, lay volunteers would be trained as counselors, in this case, receiving instruction in the basics of finances such as budgeting, debt management, socially-responsible investment, and so on. Church members involved in business, banking, and financial services would be ideal trainers and volunteers. So would your church's pastoral staff, who could teach the volunteers the biblical understanding of Christian stewardship. This would enable them to provide not only practical monetary advice, but to encourage their clients to think about their perceptions about money and "the good life" that may have gotten them in trouble in the first place. As in any counseling relationship, confidentiality would be guaranteed.

IDEA #3: Celebrate "Buy Nothing Day"

At times it seems as if Madison Avenue has stolen our religious holidays, transforming them into celebrations of unrestrained greed. As a church, help your members take back their spiritual heritage by decommercializing our sacred celebrations.

One possible vehicle for de-emphasizing the rampant materialism of the Christmas season is to join in the annual observance of "Buy Nothing Day." Since 1992, its advocates have attempted to persuade Americans not to buy anything for one whole day. The day they just happened to choose for their quixotic protest against materialism was the day after Thanksgiving, the busiest shopping day of the year. The Media Foundation, the organization that first began to promote "Buy Nothing Day," hopes to eventually succeed in implementing a global 24-hour moratorium on consumer spending.

For those who choose to participate, consider having a gathering, pot-luck, or other social event (for which you buy food and supplies ahead of time!) with an added agenda of discussing the way in which the sacred holiday can be observed with more reverence and attention to its significance to the faith. The "buy nothing" emphasis can apply to many of the religious holidays besides Christmas, such as Easter, and All Saints Day (November 1), or to historical holidays that are now mainly occasions to shop for bargains, rather than to remember or honor the contributions of those for whom the holiday was determined, such as Memorial Day, Presidents Day, or Labor Day.